THE
Comfy COZY
WITCH'S GUIDE
to Making
MAGIC
in your
EVERYDAY
LIFE

THE Comfy COZY WITCH'S GUIDE to Making MAGIC in Your EVERYDAY LIFE

JENNIE BLONDE

HarperOne

An Imprint of HarperCollinsPublishers

HarperCollins books may be purchased for educational, business, or sales promotional use. For information, please email the Special Markets Department at SPsales@harpercollins.com.

FIRST EDITION

Designed by Nancy Singer

Sigil on page 102 provided by the author

Floral line divider © Abdie/stock.adobe.com; shining moon crescent with closed eye © provectors/stock.adobe.com; medicinal herbs © nurofina/stock.adobe.com; mushrooms © kirill/stock.adobe.com; hand-drawn candles © JazzalnDigi/stock .adobe.com; cup with herbal tea © setory/stock.adobe.com; moon phases, dream catcher © Ольга E/stock.adobe.com; feathers, floral border © Maria Galybina /stock.adobe.com; runes © Wonder studio/stock.adobe.com; crystals, stars, moon © mila_okie/stock.adobe.com; books, stars © Kate Macate/stock.adobe.com; teacups © lahiru/stock.adobe.com; tea spices © Maria/stock.adobe.com; books, quill pen with ink © Vector Tradition/stock.adobe.com; fir branch © Sylfida/stock.adobe .com; bottles, moon, eye, plant, butterfly, chapter ornament burst © kssss/stock .adobe.com

Library of Congress Cataloging-in-Publication Data has been applied for.

ISBN 978-0-06-337592-5

24 25 26 27 28 LBC 5 4 3 2 1

Those who
DON'T BELIEVE IN
MAGIC
will never
FIND IT.
—Roald Dahl

CONTENTS

PART 2

MAKING YOUR *OWN* MAGIC 45

THE Comfy COZY WITCH'S GUIDE to Making MAGIC in Your EVERYDAY LIFE

INTRODUCTION

SINCE I WAS A LITTLE girl, I've been enthralled by all things witchy and magical. I dressed up as a witch for Halloween, obsessed over books in the fourth grade about ghosts and the history of witches and the occult, and truly believed I could do magic if I tried hard enough.

In 1998, I saw a book at Waldenbooks titled *To Ride a Silver Broomstick* by Silver RavenWolf. I marveled at the fact there were people out there who were real, live witches. And Silver was from Pennsylvania—just like me. I wanted so badly to resonate with that book, but for some reason I couldn't. Sure there were bits and pieces of information I plucked out of it—making my own magical journal, understanding the meanings of herbs and colors, and learning the basics of candle magic and the tarot—but much of this book was written from a Wiccan lens. For me, that label didn't fit. I wasn't interested in formal rites, rituals, and initiations—I wanted more flexibility and a practice to better fit me, and I simply couldn't find it.

My practice ebbed and flowed over the next two decades as I'd marry together bits of witchcraft through the works of Scott Cunningham, Silver RavenWolf, and Deborah Blake with my own eclectic spin. I loved all their books and borrowed many ideas for my practice, but the Wicca label still didn't resonate. So I turned to social media for more inspiration. There I found lovely displays of elaborate altar setups and perfectly curated photographs of spell work and rituals. And although I found more information and inspiration than I ever imagined, I still couldn't find my place among the picture-perfect Instagram witches—ones that seemed forced and, honestly, at times inauthentic. I knew I needed to create a practice that was right for me—not one that was ritualized or aesthetically perfect but a practice that was about nourishing myself and my family, focusing on reflection and self-care, and finding the magic in the everyday mundanities of life. A practice that was cozy and comfortable because it came from my heart.

If I couldn't find inspiration or a model for my practice out there, I decided I'd need to start creating it for myself. I cultivated my own magical practice by digging deep and finding ways to practice that aligned with what was important to me and allowed me to be flexible and not always perfect. I created an Instagram account and began posting about my process. As I interacted with other people in the witchy space—with authors, experienced practitioners, and especially new witches through Instagram and Facebook groups—I immediately sensed that same overwhelmedness and lack of belonging in others that I'd felt myself. I was confident there were hundreds, if not thousands, of people out there looking for guidance about where to begin their own practice.

In the hopes of helping people with their own practices, I decided to share what I'd learned by starting a podcast, the *Comfy Cozy Witch Podcast*. Within a month of launching my podcast, I had over twenty-five thousand downloads, and now three years in, that number has reached over one million. I was amazed and honored that my listeners responded to my authenticity and transparency, my laid-back and nonjudgmental approach to witchcraft, and my ability to make witchcraft accessible and comforting rather than intimidating. Still, I receive dozens of messages every single day (literally!) asking me for more guidance and inspiration. That's where my idea for *The Comfy Cozy Witch's Guide to Making Magic in Your Everyday Life* came from.

I want people to know that a magical practice doesn't have to be complicated, time-consuming, expensive, or perfectly curated. With the help of this book, it's my hope readers will create a practice that's all their own.

So grab yourself a cup of tea and get comfy, cozy, and witchy with me!

How to Use This Book

The Comfy Cozy Witch's Guide to Making Magic in Your Everyday Life is an interactive guide that will give you a great starting point for developing your own authentic practice and finding a place in the magical world. Drawing from years of my own magical practice, I explore the tenets of a comfy cozy practice that is authentic, approachable, and down-to-earth. This includes an introduction to witchcraft, spell craft exercises, and magical journaling prompts, as well as words of encouragement and personal anecdotes—all the tools needed to begin building a cozy, long-lasting practice where magical authenticity, comfort, and self-care are the primary focus.

The comfy cozy witch approach uses seven tenets, which I'll introduce below and spend the first part of the book exploring in depth:

🍃 ACCEPTANCE: *gentle exercises to reflect on our past journeys*

🍃 SIMPLICITY: *meditations to ground us in the present*

🍃 REFLECTION: *journal prompts to help us stay centered*

🍃 DELIGHT: *practices to find joy in community*

🍃 WARMTH: *building a cozy practice space*

🍃 BALANCE: *self-care practices, like candle magic, to replenish our inner selves*

🍃 INTUITION: *learning to listen to ourselves and connect to our guides*

My goal in bringing this book into the world is to help new and experienced practitioners alike find meaning in a magical practice and build a practice that is cozy and authentic to them. I won't be telling you what a practice *should* look like, rather, I'll be a guide of sorts, showing you what has worked for me and helping you chart your own journey into witchcraft and helping you integrate cozy magic into your everyday life. For those of you more experienced witches, it's my hope through this book you'll be reinvigorating your practice and hopefully creating a magical identity that makes sense to you.

Before we begin, it'd benefit you to either have a journal or notebook handy to take any notes you see fit, complete many of the exercises, and respond to the reflection prompts throughout this book. You can also dedicate a journal solely to this.

Each section will build upon the ones before until you've created

a witchcraft practice specifically tailored for you and your lifestyle.
The book contains the following elements:

- *Part 1 explains the basics of witchcraft for new seekers then goes into the seven tenets of a comfy cozy witchcraft practice.*

- *Part 2 covers the fundamentals of starting a practice from the inside out, exploring magical journaling, meditating, self-care, gratitude, and intuition—parts of the craft that require you to dig deep inside yourself. These inner-magic and outer-magic activities for each tenet will help you discover what it is you want to get out of a magical practice because it's important to know your expectations and wants and needs for a spiritual practice before jumping into the more tangible goodies.*

- *I offer inner-magic exercises, which include journaling prompts, guided meditations, and activities, that ask you to discover and reflect upon your inner magical needs before moving on to the outer-magic exercises.*

- *The outer-magic sections discuss the more tangible parts of a magical practice—your sacred space, altar space, magical tools, hearth and home, and nature—and guide you in curating an outer practice that makes sense to you. Through more prompts, meditations, and exercises, you'll discover what outer magic means to you and how you can best utilize these elements to fit your practice.*

- *In the final chapters, you'll bring together your discoveries from the tenets and corresponding activities to begin piecing together your own magical practice. I'll lead you through creating a daily ritual that works with your schedule and life, we'll explore divination tools and intentional magic, you'll create spells and rituals, and you'll discover what a cozy practice means to you and how you can tap into your magic in one form or another every single day.*

For more experienced practitioners wanting to level up their practice or reinvigorate their craft, or for those craving a shift in their magic, throughout the book I'll offer additional exercises I've labeled Level Up activities designed to do just that. You can treat this as a choose-your-own-exercise type of interactive guidebook.

All prompts and activities are cozy in nature and created with time and ease in mind. Nowhere will I ask you to spend hours upon hours journaling and meditating or completing magical exercises that require dozens of hard-to-find items. Ideally, you'll read this book and complete the corresponding exercises in sequential order, taking your time; however, if you'd rather pick and choose particular sections or specific prompts and exercises to complete, that's fine too. I am a huge advocate for learning and practicing however you see fit.

In the end, I want everyone who reads this book—no matter your previous experience—to walk away with a practice that's not only authentic to you but one that leaves you feeling comfy, cozy, and witchy.

Let's get started!

Where Do We Begin?

Before we dive into the tenets of a comfy cozy magical practice, let's get into the basics. If you're a more experienced practitioner, feel free to jump to chapter 1.

What Is Witchcraft?

If you ask ten witches what witchcraft is, you'll get eleven different answers. Witchcraft is so personal in nature and means something different to pretty much every person you ask. Walking your path as a magical person—a witch, a healer, or whichever word or language appeals most to you—is to search for something deeper in yourself and in the universe. It's about working with the Earth, the moon, your spiritual guides (ancestors, deities, angels, and so on), and yourself in order to become who you are meant to be. It's about using your intuition, finding stillness in the chaos, and working with energy in all its forms. Most important, it's about finding and *creating* magic in your everyday life and acknowledging the magic in, well, everything, especially within yourself.

THE ELEMENTS

Magic truly is all around us, and we tend to take that for granted. Especially when it comes to the four natural elements—air, fire, water, and earth. The basis to a magical practice is knowing the elements and how they relate to the various parts of our lives. Everything we encounter possesses qualities that correspond with one or more of the four elements. And we're reminded of the magic that surrounds us by recognizing that the everyday things we do—the fire of our candle, the air we breathe, the water we bathe in, the earth we walk on—are components of our spiritual practice. Let's take a closer look.

AIR: Air is associated with the direction east and the season of spring. It rules communication and thoughts. Ways to connect with the air element is through lighting incense, cleaning your home, breathing deeply, practicing meditation or yoga, speaking aloud magical charms, magical journaling and writing, collecting feathers, planting fragrant herbs and flowers, and smelling the air when you walk outside.

EARTH: Earth is associated with the winter season and the cardinal north. Its colors are green, brown, and black, and the animals closely associated with earth are the bear, dog, deer, and fox. Earth rules our physical bodies, nature, animals, death, and the practical things in life like money. Ways to connect with earth are by getting out in nature, touching a creek, stream, or ocean, practicing mindfulness and meditation, walking barefoot on the land, and disconnecting from technology.

FIRE: The element of fire is connected to the summer season and the direction south. Its colors are red, orange, crimson, and bright yellow, while stones associated with fire are ruby, red jasper, bloodstone, and garnet. Fire rules creativity, passion, your blood, and healing, and its animals are the dragon, lion, horse, and snake. You can connect to fire by lighting a candle, performing candle magic, moving your body, gazing at the stars, basking in the sun's light, or sipping on a hot beverage.

WATER: Water is associated with the direction west and the season of fall. Its colors are blue, turquoise, green, and gray—colors you'd associate with the ocean. Animals of water are fish, dolphins, cats, and sea mammals, and water rules our emotions, intuition, cleansing, and fertility. You can connect with the element of water by bathing, consecrating magical tools, practicing self-care rituals, journaling about your emotions, doing something for self-relaxation, or going for a swim.

SPIRIT: Surprise! There is actually a fifth element, and that is spirit. Spirit, also known as the element ether, is associated with all other elements, the heavens, and other realms. Its animals are the mystical unicorns, chameleons, and spiders; while spirit's crystals are amethyst, moonstone, aura quartz, and clear quartz. Spirit's a bridge to everything known and the best way to connect with spirit is through divination, working with your ancestors and guides, and spell work and meditation.

ELEMENTS IN NATURE

One of the best places to connect with the elements is through nature. We step outside and see the fire of the sun, the water of lakes and streams, the air in the wind that blows through our hair, and the earth of the grass below our feet. Because such a large part of a witch's magical practice involves caring for and communing with nature, it's important for us to find ways to connect to it. Not only does connecting with nature bring us closer to our magic, it's also integral to our mental health and general well-being. I know that many of us live in cities or towns that lack green spaces or access to mountains and the sea, but there are things you can do to tap into nature and the magic of the elements wherever you reside.

DISPLAY ART: *Even if you're concrete-locked and lacking green where you live, you can still tap into the calming properties of nature through images. Hang a picture of the ocean in your bedroom. Place a painting of a forest in your office. Print out a favorite image of woodland creatures and display it in your kitchen. Look at these pictures daily to connect with nature in a new way.*

COLLECT STONES AND STICKS: *My dad used to get upset with me when I was a child because I brought home every stick and stone I could find. I'd place them in my pockets and when he'd put my laundry in the dryer, the stones would* cling *and* clang *and dent our laundry machine. Picking up stones shouldn't end in childhood. Keep your eyes open for stones on your path that call out to you. Scoop them up and take them home. Place them in a location where you'll see them every day.*

BRING IN FLOWERS: *It you don't have access to flower gardens or local parks, head to your nearest florist or grocery store and grab a small bouquet of flowers of your choosing. Flowers represent all elements as their fragrance corresponds to air, they grow in the sun (fire), they need water for growth (water), and they spring from the ground (earth). Not only that, but many flowers are connected with spirit through their connections to the divine.*

GATHER FEATHERS: *Bringing feathers into your home is another great way to bring the beauty of nature inside. After cleansing your feathers by gently spraying rubbing alcohol on them, place them on your altar (which we'll talk about in chapter 8), bedside table, or anywhere you see fit. Spiritually speaking, feathers in our path are often considered messages from our angels. However, they can also* be a message from a passed loved one or from your spirit guides. Different colored feathers indicate various types of messages.

🖎 BRING IN SEASHELLS: *Like flowers, shells are connected to all elements and remind us of the beauty and fragility of nature, and their shape represents a connection to femininity. Decorate your dresser, bathroom counter, or altar with shells to connect with the energy of water and the sea.*

FEATHER MEANINGS

Have you ever noticed feathers showing up in your life over and over again—on your front doorstep, while out on a walk, painted on the side of a building, or even mentioned in a book you're reading? No matter what form the feather comes in, these beautiful items often carry messages to us from our guides—angels, passed loved ones, deities, and so on. Finding a feather on your path is a way these guides communicate with you. Below is an overview of feather colors and what they represent.

- **WHITE**: peace, security, ancestors. These are a sign someone is watching over you. An ancestor is letting you know everything is okay on the other side.

- BLACK: protection, rebirth. A black feather is a sign of warning and reminds you to trust your intuition. It's also a sign a new beginning is coming.

- GRAY: neutrality and peace. A gray feather signifies peace is coming to your life after a time of tumult.

- BLUE: peace, communication, psychic awareness. A blue feather tells you to tune in to your intuitive and psychic abilities. It also reminds you to speak your truth.

- BROWN: grounding, pause. A brown feather signifies a need to ground and to wait for clarity before making any decisions.

- YELLOW: enlightenment, joy. A yellow feather is a sign that you're on the right path to enlightenment and happiness.

The Eight Seasonal Celebrations

As a comfy cozy witch, I am in the peak of my magic when I am celebrating and honoring the eight seasonal celebrations or sabbats. Although the term *sabbat* got its start in Wicca—a God and Goddess initiative-based practice—many modern witches celebrate these festivals that honor the birth-life-death cycle and the harvest cycle. These festivals also include the four main solar events of the solstices and equinoxes. Honoring these eight points in the year is a great way to connect with not only the seasons but with your innate magic. My family and I celebrate these eight festivities through seasonal food, small family rituals, and time spent observing the rhythmic changes in nature. Although by no means a necessity for your own practice, somehow honoring these festivals will have you feeling more in tune with the seasonal rhythms. Here's a handy guide so you can mark your calendar ahead of time and be prepared to celebrate!

SAMHAIN: OCTOBER 31—NOVEMBER 1

Considered the Witches' New Year, Samhain is a favorite among magic makers. During this festival, passed loved ones (family, friends, and animals) are honored. The veil between our realm and the spiritual realm is at its thinnest this time of year, so it's perfect for connecting to those who have passed. Samhain is also a great time to do any divination work. You can honor Samhain by creating an ancestor altar, going on cemetery walks, carving and decorating gourds and pumpkins, and sharing family stories.

COLORS: black, red, and orange
GEMSTONES: carnelian, obsidian, bloodstone, and onyx

Magical intentions include ancestors, crone wisdom, death, divination, and introspection.

YULE/WINTER SOLSTICE: DECEMBER 20—23

Yule is a festival that begins on the longest and darkest night of the year. Although Yule and winter solstice festivities celebrate the return of the light as the days slowly begin to get longer, it also marks the beginning of the coldest months ahead. Festivities of Yule focus on the fire and the hearth, and it won't surprise you to learn that many cultures around the world have their own celebrations of the return of the light—Christmas, Saturnalia, Hanukkah, and Kwanzaa. Candles are symbolic of this light, and the evergreen wreaths that so many display on their doors symbolize the circle of life.

COLORS: green, red, white, silver, and gold
GEMSTONES: ruby, moss agate, and snowflake obsidian

You can honor this sabbat by making a Yule altar, creating and burning a Yule log, decorating an evergreen tree, exchanging gifts made from nature, and having a bonfire.

IMBOLC: FEBRUARY 1—2

Imbolc is a cross-quarter celebration—one that takes place halfway between a solstice and an equinox. It is the first of three fertility festivals where spring is beginning to unfurl in the ground, even if we can't see it yet. Because this marks the time just before spring, Imbolc is a great time to think about growth and change and what intentions you want to set for the coming weeks. Imbolc is the final push through winter, and it's celebrated for and embodied by newness, creation, increasing love in the household, and creating prosperity and abundance for you and your loved ones.

COLORS: white, silver, green, and yellow

GEMSTONES: snowy quartz, goldstone, fire agate, and ruby

You can honor Imbolc by crafting straw goddess dolls, hosting a feast, cleaning your home, and decorating your altar with Imbolc corresponding colors, stones, and décor.

OSTARA/SPRING EQUINOX: MARCH 19—22

Ostara marks the spring equinox, a time of year with equal day and night, light and dark. Like the fall equinox, which we'll chat about soon, this is a time of balance—cool and warmth, light and dark, female and male energies, death and rebirth, inner and outer self, and the physical and spiritual world. As a fire festival celebrating the ever-returning sun, Ostara celebrates rebirth, renewal, growth, and new beginnings.

COLORS: pastel pink, yellow, blue, and green

GEMSTONES: amethyst, citrine, rose quartz, clear quartz, and aquamarine

You can celebrate this sabbat by releasing what no longer serves you, watching birds in your local lands, dyeing Ostara eggs, planting herb and flower seeds, walking in nature, or journaling about changes you'd like to see in yourself.

BELTANE: MAY 1—2

Beltane is the third of the fertility sabbats and falls midway between the spring equinox and summer solstice. Also celebrated as May Day, this festival is known for music, fragrance, passion, and abundance.

Beltane celebrates the full birth of spring as the land has turned green with grass, flowers are in bloom, bees are buzzing around, and birds are chirping on windowsills. It celebrates youth, beauty, sensuality, vitality, and health.

COLORS: green, pink, red, and orange

GEMSTONES: amber, rose quartz, carnelian, amethyst, and emerald

You can celebrate this festival by working with fairies; making fairy cake; creating a mini maypole; casting spells for love, self-love, and fertility; and indulging in a self-love ritual bath.

LITHA / SUMMER SOLSTICE: JUNE 20—24

Also known as Midsummer, this sabbat celebrates the longest day of the year when the sun is at its peak energy. This is when the earth is at its most fertile and the landscape is vibrant with color. Gardens are being tended to and herbs, fruits, and vegetables are harvested and consumed. At this time of year summer is in full swing and light and the sun are honored.

COLORS: red, blue, orange, gold, and vibrant yellow

GEMSTONES: diamond, emerald, jade, and carnelian

You can celebrate Litha by hosting a bonfire celebration, making floral wreaths and crowns, building a fairy garden, and gathering herbs to dry for recipes. This is a great time to focus on fertility and life, manifestation and power, and the strength and success of abundance.

LUGHNASADH/LAMMAS: AUGUST 1–2

The first of three harvest festivals, Lughnasadh (named in honor of the Celtic Sun God Lugh) celebrates grain and the beginning of the harvest season. As another cross-quarter day, Lughnasadh marks the midpoint between the summer solstice and the autumn equinox (my personal favorite). Historically, this was the time of year when ancient peoples would cut the first sheaves of grain to make loaves of bread.

COLORS: yellow, gold, brown, orange, and green
GEMSTONES: citrine, tiger's-eye, peridot, and rhodonite

This is a great festival to focus on what intentions have come to fruition over the past few months and is a wonderful time for baking homemade breads, crafting corn dollies, volunteering in nature, or going on a nature walk.

MABON/AUTUMN EQUINOX: SEPTEMBER 21–23

My personal favorite turn on the wheel, the autumn equinox marks the start of the autumn season, and celestially, it's another day of balance, with equal parts light and dark. Also known as the Witch's Thanksgiving, Mabon is when many give thanks for what the earth has provided in nourishment, thanks for family and friends, and thanks for animal friends. To me, this is the coziest of sabbats as the weather where I live turns cooler. It's a time to reflect on what the year has brought so far and a reminder to be grateful for all I have. It's also the time of year to prepare for and welcome in the darker months.

COLORS: traditional hues of fall—burnt orange, deep red, burgundy, violet, and purple

GEMSTONES: citrine, golden healer, and bloodstone

FOODS: apples, nuts, dried fruits, breads, squash, seeds, wine, and cider

You can celebrate this sabbat by hosting a Mabon feast, completing gratitude rituals, decorating for the autumn season, and baking, as well as celebrating your family, hearth, and home.

Moon Phases

Throughout history, the moon has held a powerful mystical significance for many magic seekers. Each moon phase gives off different energies, so many practitioners plan their spell work and rituals around the lunar calendar. Living a life aligned with the moon is all about being aware of its cycles and how to work with the various types of energy the moon puts off and how that energy affects your physical, emotional, and spiritual self.

The moon reflects our intuition, our inner knowing, and our moods. When we work with it, we're choosing to recognize and honor those parts of ourselves. Before getting into the particulars of each phase, here are a few ways to tap into the moon's energy no matter the phase:

Start a mood journal where you reflect on your emotions at various parts of the moon cycle. Notice the ebb and flow of your own mood, emotions, and energy throughout the month and record how they correspond to the phases of the moon.

- *Research the astrology associated with the month and how the signs of the zodiac impact the moon cycle.*

- *Simply stare at the moon, taking notice of its shape and phase. Add this to your journal or calendar to keep track of the phases over the course of a cycle.*

- *Get to know the various qualities of each moon phase and how best to work with them.*

- *Get outside and find a spot where the moon shines down on you. Bask in its glow, allowing it to fill you with radiance and light.*

NEW MOON

This is the start of a new lunar cycle. It's the perfect time for setting intentions and for checking in with yourself emotionally. Although we can barely see the moon in the sky, know it's there and its energy is waiting to be worked with.

KEYWORDS: fresh start and intentions

MAGICAL WORKINGS: new love or romance, new job, better communication, plans of any kind, new diet, fertility, and attraction

WAXING CRESCENT

This phase is a time to really dig in and do the work to manifest what you want to attract in your life. Don't be afraid to get your hands dirty and do the spell work to manifest your desires.

KEYWORDS: manifesting and action

MAGICAL WORKINGS: creativity and inspiration, healing and health issues, money and abundance, business growth, and relationship growth

FIRST QUARTER MOON

The first quarter moon provides the perfect opportunity to evaluate your intentions and manifestation progress. If you need to redirect, now is the time to do so.

KEYWORDS: balance, perseverance, and overcoming

MAGICAL WORKINGS: creativity, overcoming obstacles, and healing

WAXING GIBBOUS

This is a time when your feelings and emotions may get the best of you, especially if you're not yet seeing progress in the intentions you've set. Do a self-care check-in at this time.

KEYWORDS: endurance and refinement

MAGICAL WORKINGS: courage, determination, and inspiration

FULL MOON

This is when the moon is completely illuminated by the reflection of the sun. Our emotions are at their peak power, so it's a great time for magical working. This is also an excellent time to practice gratitude.

KEYWORDS: magic, fulfillment, and gratitude
MAGICAL WORKINGS: divination, protection of house and home, removing barriers, emotional healing, and moon water creation

WANING GIBBOUS MOON

The full moon is slowly beginning to decrease and you may feel the need to recharge from the emotions of the full moon at this time. Begin thinking about any people or emotions you want to release.

KEYWORDS: reflect and release
MAGICAL WORKINGS: removing negativity and calming anxiety

LAST QUARTER MOON

This is the phase to evaluate what no longer serves you. From this cycle on, think about releasing bad habits and energy that doesn't serve you.

KEYWORDS: balance and boundaries
MAGICAL WORKINGS: setting boundaries, warding from psychic attacks, and banishing bad habits

WANING CRESCENT

The moon is finishing out its current cycle and preparing for the next. For many this phase can be low-energy and a great time for introspection.

KEYWORDS: recharge and self-care
MAGICAL WORKINGS: self-care rituals, calming anxiety, and blessing
the home

DARK MOON

This phase isn't recognized by many. It's that slight moment in time when the moon is entirely in shadow in the sky. This is a period of stillness, rest, and deep introspection.

KEYWORDS: quiet, still, and reflection
MAGICAL WORKINGS: shadow work and divination

Crystals

A staple in many witches' spaces is crystals. There are countless books out there on crystals, crystal magic, crystal healing, and so on, and you'll notice that not every source says the same thing about how to use them. What the sources can agree on is that crystals have been around and used for millions and millions of years, and they've been used in magical workings and healing work for just as long. Crystals enhance our lives by bringing in protection, healing, happiness, abundance, and more to you and/or to those you use crystals on. Place crystals you like—either raw crystals, tumbled stones, shaped and/or polished ones—around your home, workspace, and even in your potted plants to attract all sorts of energies. We'll chat more about this later in part 2!

I have crystals placed sporadically around my home—some crystals I've chosen because I was drawn to them, others I chose because I liked the way they look, and some I've chosen due to their magical and energetic properties. I believe that however we acquire crystals—whether gifted, intuitively chosen, or chosen because they're *pretty*—we're meant to possess them.

For reference, here are some common crystals and their common magical and energetic uses.

CLEAR QUARTZ

This is the stone of happiness, success, and health. It's known as the "master healer" and as an amplifier stone, as it amplifies the healing energies of stones around it. A staple in most witch's cabinets, clear quartz also enhances intuition and psychic ability.

ROSE QUARTZ

Rose quartz, also known as the "love stone" with its light pink hue, is best for workings dealing with love, friendship, self-love, compassion, and healing. Keep rose quartz on your bedside table to bring a loving relationship into your space, or keep it in your bathroom to remind you of your innate beauty.

AMETHYST

Amethyst is not only one of the most abundant crystals out there, but it's also one of the most spiritual. A versatile stone, amethyst is known to help calm, bring peace, heal, connect to spirit guides and higher self, and deepen meditation. It makes a lovely piece of jewelry that when worn can add a boost of protection and balance.

CITRINE

Citrine is a popular stone used to enhance joy, creativity, learning, and work life. Citrine is also a crystal to work with when abundance is desired, especially when it comes to money. Citrine pushes its user to work hard, persevere, and assist in making intentions come to fruition.

AVENTURINE

Known for its ability to create new opportunities, give good luck, and bring prosperity, aventurine is a popular stone for obvious reasons. It's known as the "stone of opportunity" for good reason. It can also soothe anger, anxiety, and nervous energy, as well as balance erratic emotions. Make sure to cleanse this stone often.

TURQUOISE

One of the oldest known stones, turquoise is a powerful crystal that promotes clear communication, success, leadership, and abundance. Turquoise is also known to help mend a broken relationship and connect to passed loved ones. Wearing a turquoise necklace in particular

CLEARING AND ACTIVATING CRYSTALS

Unless you've mined and polished and shaped your own stones and crystals by hand, most likely someone else's energy has come in contact with your collection of gems. Even if you've handpicked your stones, they probably came wrapped in some sort of synthetic protective material, packaged by others, handled by others, and interacted with all sorts of energy throughout the process.

No matter the energy your stones have picked up before coming to you, it's important to cleanse the stones before use. You can do this a variety of ways. You can soak nonporous stones in salt water or hold them in a fresh stream of running water. You can place the stones in a large bowl of sea salt overnight then gently brush the salt from their crevices. You can let them rest overnight in the moonlight, or you can cleanse them with incense smoke. You can also cleanse them by placing them on a plate of selenite or by ringing a bell above them to do a little sound clearing.

Once you've used one of the methods to cleanse your stones, it's time to activate them, which prepares them for magical use. Like imbuing your intention into other magical tools, which we'll discuss in detail later, simply hold the crystal(s) in your left hand and cover it with your right. Either speak your intention aloud or in your head, directing that intentional energy toward the stone.

promotes clear communication and calm due to its location close to the throat chakra.

FLUORITE

Fluorite is a popular stone for protection, cleansing, and healing. It protects its user on both a physical and psychic level as well as helps connecting to one's true self. When you are in need of physical or emotional healing, wear a piece of jewelry made from fluorite. And this stone is just plain gorgeous when held up to light.

LAPIS LAZULI

One of my favorite stones, lapis lazuli enhances intuitive awareness and psychic powers. It has a deep, royal blue color with flecks of sparkling pyrite pieces and has been known to ease headaches as well as keep anxiety at bay. Hold a piece of lapis lazuli to your third eye to assist in clairvoyant communication.

LABRADORITE

A favorite among magical people, labradorite is known as the "stone of magic." It's a popular crystal for witches, healers, and those who are seeking self-transformation, self-discovery, and a spiritual practice. It also is a protective stone that you can use when doing boundary-setting work or when traveling between realms.

BLACK OBSIDIAN

A powerful stone for protection, black obsidian absorbs stress and other negative energies. Place obsidian pieces around your home to ensure physical and psychic protection. But make sure to regularly cleanse this stone by placing it in a bowl of salt, burying it outside in dirt, or using a smoke cleanse, as it soaks in a variety of energies.

Chakras

I want to quickly touch on the seven main chakras, or energy centers, of the body as I will be mentioning them throughout the book and want you to know what I'm talking about. Originating from Eastern philosophy, these seven energy centers run down the middle of the body. Energy flows through them and around the body, and when it's flowing freely you feel balanced, healthy, and connected to your magic. If any of these centers become blocked, you may feel stifled in areas of your life or even unwell.

The chakras both absorb and transmit energy, so your energy can impact others just as their energy can impact yours. Here's a brief overview of the chakras:

> CROWN: *Located above the head, this chakra corresponds to higher knowledge, connection to the spiritual realm, and mental activity.*
>> COLORS: pale purple and white
>> CRYSTALS: clear quartz, selenite, and rainbow moonstone

THIRD EYE: *Located between your eyes, this chakra is associated with intuition, inner knowing, and clear-sightedness.*

> COLOR: violet
>
> CRYSTALS: amethyst, angelite, and lapis lazuli

THROAT: *This energy center, located in your throat area, corresponds with the ability to communicate your ideas, thoughts, and feelings and to speak your truth.*

> COLOR: blue
>
> CRYSTALS: turquoise, aquamarine, sodalite, and blue kyanite

HEART: *Located in the center of your chest, the heart chakra is all about love, compassion, empathy, and connection to family.*

> COLORS: green and pink
>
> CRYSTALS: jade, green aventurine, malachite, rose quartz, and rhodonite

SOLAR PLEXUS: *Above the navel in your torso is the solar plexus chakra, which controls your confidence and self-esteem.*

> COLOR: yellow
>
> CRYSTALS: tiger's-eye, citrine, yellow calcite, and amber

SACRAL: *Located in the lower abdomen, the sacral chakra is associated with creativity, sensuality, passion, and at times, intuition (gut feelings).*

> COLOR: orange
>
> CRYSTALS: carnelian, orange calcite, and sunstone

ROOT: *Located at the base of the spine, the root chakra controls family matters, grounding, security, and protection.*

> COLOR: red
>
> CRYSTALS: red jasper, bloodstone, smoky quartz, and garnet

What We've Learned Here Is Just a Start!

There are so many other topics in the witchcraft arena that I could discuss, but that would take up an entirely separate book. What I do recommend is to do your own research in the areas of a magical practice that appeal to you. If you're drawn to divination, research the various types in depth and then practice. (Note: We will be chatting about divination in chapter 10!) If your interest is piqued as you read about crystals, grab a few books on crystals or head to your local New Age shop to interact with them in person. Personally, I connect most with stones if I can touch them myself. If you're curious about astrology, working with angels, connecting with your spirit guides, magic making with herbs and plants, and more, whatever you do, focus on depth over breadth. You don't want to rush your learning. Ease yourself into your magical practice. Interacting with the tenets in the next few chapters and completing the inner- and outer-magic exercises throughout this book will help you do just that!

Tenets of Comfy Cozy Witchcraft/Magic

The first question I often get asked about my practice is, "What exactly does it mean to be a comfy cozy witch?" A lot of people like the idea of both comfort and witchcraft, but wonder how it can be defined. And honestly, there isn't a single definition for *comfy cozy witchcraft*, just as there isn't a single definition for *green witchcraft* or *hedge witchcraft* or for *magic* in general. If you listen to my podcast, you know I'm not a big fan of putting a solid definition to anyone's practice, as it varies from person to person. Instead, I'd rather give my comfy cozy practice a variety of words and phrases to best encapsulate what it is. So what I have for you isn't a definition, rather a series of tenets, or guiding principles, that encapsulate comfy cozy witchcraft.

These principles of self-exploration and discovery—acceptance, simplicity, reflection, delight, warmth, balance, intuition—helped guide my own craft, and it's my hope they inspire you, whether you're someone who is new to magic or a more experienced witch looking to reinvigorate your practice. At the end of each tenet, I've included an exercise for inner magical work and discovery and an exercise for outer magic. Where appropriate I've also included questions for you to ponder. Although we haven't yet talked about magical journaling (coming up soon—in chapter 3), I urge you to grab a notebook, take a moment to reflect upon the guided questions and/or exercises, and try answering them as honestly as possible.

1

TENET

ACCEPTANCE

BEFORE WE CAN MOVE INTO the tangible elements of witchcraft—the spell work, tools, ritual creation, etc.—it's important to discover what is important to us and how we can prepare our mind, body, and spirit for a magical practice. In this section, I'll introduce you to what I feel are important aspects to discovering your inner magic. I'll offer journal prompts for reflection and growth as well as exercises to discover your inner magical needs to create your own path. We'll discuss self-care, meditation and grounding, intuition, practicing gratitude, and intuition—all aspects of our mindful inner magic.

As a reminder, for each of the tenets we'll also explore *outer magic* connected to them. Included in the outer-magic exercises will be things you can *do* and put into *action* to honor and further explore each tenet. You'll complete meditations, practice basic spell work, make plans to meet other like-minded people, and begin building a cozy magical place to practice.

Acceptance

One thing many magic seekers have in common is the inability to find acceptance in a traditional spiritual community. For centuries witches have been persecuted. Between 1450 and 1750 alone, more than one hundred thousand people in colonial America and in Europe, mostly women, were prosecuted for practicing magic. These women were healers, many unmarried, who posed a threat to men and to religious practices of the time. We've come a long way since then. And although witchcraft is much more accepted nowadays, many new seekers can't seem to find their place within the community. The last thing we need when starting on a spiritual journey is to feel like an outsider.

I know when I came back to my practice, it was difficult to find my space among the curated Instagram feeds and structured practices, not to mention the varied, albeit strong, opinions on what witchcraft *should* look like. What I've come to realize though is your practice is yours and yours alone, and because of this, I knew a tenet of comfy cozy witchcraft had to be acceptance. An acceptance of others and acceptance of yourself.

You shouldn't be worried if you're "not witchy enough" or don't look or dress like the stereotypical witch or the ones you see on your social media feeds. I mean, my go-to getup is yoga pants and a baggy, cozy sweater. And you also shouldn't be concerned with those out there telling others they're practicing witchcraft wrong. In my eyes, there's no wrong way to have a magical practice because each practice is individual.

And judgment doesn't always come from outside sources. Oftentimes we judge ourselves and our practice more harshly than others and their practices, and so you want to come to your craft with an attitude of self-acceptance, compassion, and grace. A comfy cozy witch is one that is accepting of others and accepting of themselves, wherever they are in their journey. In that respect, it's a practice that's nonjudgmental and one that feels right to you. When we force ourselves to fit into a mold or try to be what we perceive through others as *witchy*, we aren't being authentic. So it makes sense that the first tenet of comfy cozy magic is to accept yourself for where you are on your spiritual journey and not worry about the thoughts and opinions of others.

COLORS FOR ACCEPTANCE: white, yellow, beige, and pink

CRYSTALS FOR ACCEPTANCE: amber, amethyst, aquamarine, clear quartz, and rose quartz

QUESTIONS TO PONDER: What has turned me off about beginning a witchcraft practice in the past? What would it feel like to be accepted by the magical community? How can I be more accepting of magic within myself and others?

-✵ INNER MAGIC ✵-

Spiritual Journey Timeline

What you'll need

Journal or notebook

Writing utensil

Method

For this exercise I want you to think about your spiritual development and journey over the years. Go back as far as you can remember. Maybe you grew up going to Sunday school each weekend, or maybe your parents forced you to attend church with them. During your teenage years, did you step away from spirituality? Or perhaps this is the very beginning for you. Whichever it is document your spiritual journey. See if you can connect events with the various milestones in your journey. Oftentimes we seek out something larger than ourselves in moments of turmoil, stress, or unease.

⊰⊱ OUTER MAGIC ⊰⊱

Acceptance Guided Meditation

This guided meditation is one to do if you're looking for spiritual connection and self-acceptance. This will be especially useful to those newer to witchcraft, but it can also be completed by anyone who has felt a bit disconnected from their practice. Feel free to record yourself reading this meditation and play it aloud when you're ready to complete it.

What you'll need

Candle in the color and scent of your choosing (one that makes you feel comfortable and calm)

Candle-safe dish or holder

Lighter or matches

Journal or notebook

Writing utensil

Method

1. Sit in a quiet area of your house, out in nature, or in your sacred space. Place your candle on a candle-safe dish and light it. Place

your right hand on your chest, just over your heart, and your left hand on your stomach, over your solar plexus area. Take three deep breaths and while you do so, focus on nothing but those breaths.

2. Close your eyes and say the mantras that appeal to you aloud, three times each. Pause between each mantra and notice if any thoughts, smells, visuals, or sounds come up.

I seek a connection with the divine.
I am open to guidance in my practice.
I am deserving of self-care and compassion.
I am proud of myself for beginning my spiritual journey.

3. When you're finished, journal about this meditative experience. What did you see? Hear? Feel? Smell? Touch? By chance, did any messages come through?

·✦ LEVEL UP ✦·

Your Spiritual Journey Timeline

For those of you who've practiced for quite some time, I want you to reflect on where you've been over the years on your witchcraft journey. Create a timeline documenting the beginning of your magical journey to the present. Think about major shifts in your practice and what was going on in your life during those shifts. Take this a step further and document how you envision the next five, ten, fifteen, and twenty years of your journey. Where have you been in the past? And where do you see your practice taking you in the future?

2

TENET

SIMPLICITY

THE SECOND TENET OF COMFY cozy witchcraft is simplicity. The simpler I can make my rituals, my spells, and my practice, the more likely I am to complete them and come back to them day after day. There's no need for complication as complication oftentimes leads to feeling overwhelmed and burnout.

I see many who are new to witchcraft struggle to maintain a practice because they do too much too soon—whether that's reading books on every witchcraft topic possible in a short amount of time; signing up for tarot reading, Reiki healing, and mediumship classes in one shot; or jumping into opening a witchy business a month after being introduced to witchcraft. My advice is to take things slow. Think about what drew you to witchcraft in the first place. Find a topic in the witchcraft realm that appeals to you—herbal magic, witchcraft history, astrology, crystal magic, and so on—and focus on that one topic for a while before moving on to the next. I'm a big fan of depth over breadth, especially in the beginning.

The simplicity tenet applies to magical tools as well. There is no need to go out and purchase hundreds of dollars' worth of crystals and card decks and altar décor, just as there's no need to perform an elaborate ten-step daily ritual that takes up hours of time. To continue a practice, it should flow easily, naturally, and seamlessly within your day. Finding magic in the small things—the birds first chirping in spring, a pot of basil sprouting, the full moon shining, a meal on the Autumn Equinox—can be just as impactful (and less time consuming) than those formal rites and rituals you read about.

COLORS FOR SIMPLICITY: pastels, white, and gray
CRYSTALS FOR SIMPLICITY: green and blue calcite, aquamarine, citrine, and clear quartz

Meditation and Grounding in Magic

One of the simplest ways to grow your spiritual practice is through setting up a grounding routine through meditation. As I've said many times before on the podcast, grounding exercises and meditation are a basis for magical working, so it's important you are skilled in them. I've been meditating consistently for more than a decade, and I wish I'd started sooner as it's completely transformed my practice. I know many people are turned off by meditation because they struggle to quiet their mind and remain still. But I'm here to tell you that the only way to get into a meditation practice is by doing it. If you're just starting out in meditation, look for guided meditations that are narrated;

this is a great alternative to guiding yourself in the overwhelming quiet. You can also record yourself narrating a meditation. One of the best apps for beginning meditation is Insight Timer. It's a free app filled with guided meditations on a variety of topics—sleeping meditations, sabbat connection meditations, mindfulness practices, connections to your spirit guides, and so much more. I personally love many of the guided spirit guide meditations and anything by the amazingly witchy Sarah Robinson of Sentia Yoga! Jon Kabat-Zinn's books, videos, meditations app, and masterclasses are also amazing resources if you're just delving into meditation.

INNER MAGIC

Spiritual Journey Nonnegotiables

As I said, oftentimes people tend to dive right into an overwhelming number of topics when they're just beginning their spiritual/magical journey. I always urge not to do too much too soon, as that leads to burnout. To help get your priorities in line for your spiritual practice, complete this simple exercise. Use the space below to list out some of your spiritual nonnegotiables—topics and interests you want to learn about sooner rather than later as you discover your practice. Now narrow that list down to your top three. What makes each topic so appealing to you?

OUTER MAGIC

Grounding Exercise

Since grounding truly is the basis of any magical working, it's important to understand the variety of ways there are to ground. For the next three days, I'd like you to choose one grounding technique from the following list to complete daily. Make sure you journal how you feel *before* and *after* you complete the grounding exercise.

* Find a body of running water and place your hands in it. Focus on how the water feels on your fingertips, on your palms, on the back of your hands, and on your forearms.

* Take a five-to-ten-minute walk in nature without any music or distractions. Focus on the sounds that you hear as you walk . . . your feet on the ground, the birds chirping, the soft breaking of branches and rustling of trees.

* Go outside, take your shoes and socks off, and stand barefoot on the ground. Imagine a tree root growing up from the earth and winding around your body in a gentle hug.

* Mindfully sip on a cup of tea or other hot beverage, letting yourself savor each sip. Notice the taste of the drink, how it feels in your mouth and throat, and how it makes you feel emotionally.

LEVEL UP

Present Moment Exercise

So much of our lives are built around to-do lists, work deadlines, and the stressors of home. We often forget to be mindful, intentional, and thoughtful, which can make us bystanders in our own lives rather than active participants. When you're feeling disconnected from yourself, run down, or close to burnout, complete the following exercise.

What you'll need

Pillow or cushion (optional)

Your favorite candle or incense

Candle-safe dish or incense holder

Lighter or matches

Crystal of your choosing

Method

1. Take a seat in an area with little to no distractions. Feel free to sit on a pillow or cushion of some kind for this exercise.
2. Place your favorite scented candle on a candle-safe dish and light it. Hold on to the crystal.
3. Take three deep breaths, focusing on the quiet that envelops you. Allow the scent of your candle, the ambient noise, and any sensations you feel fill your senses. If you're feeling discomfort anywhere, acknowledge that and then bring your attention back to your senses.
4. Hold the crystal tightly in your fist and bring that hand to the center of your chest, fingers against you.
5. Begin chanting a deep *Ommmm*. Close your eyes as you do so, and focus on the sound of the chant and the vibration in your chest. Imagine the sound waves flowing out from your chest, through the crystal, and into your space, pushing any stale energy away with each chant.
6. Chant until you've imagined all that energy drifting away, and come back to your breath. Notice again the scent of your candle or incense, the ambient noise, and any sensations in your body.
7. Slowly open your eyes and notice how you're feeling. A sense of calm and renewal should wash over you as you close the meditation.

3

REFLECTION

ONE OF THE KEYS TO a comfy cozy practice is reflecting on your spiritual journey and checking in with your magic. Since we all change over time, it's no surprise our spiritual beliefs and practices do too. It's important to note these shifts in ourselves, in our spiritual practices, and in our values and what we find important to our growth. My number one way of reflecting on my practice is by keeping a written record of it in the form of a magical journal.

When you first think about magical journals, I'm sure your mind goes to the Book of Shadows or the grimoire. Traditionally, a Book of Shadows is where witches would keep a recording of their magical workings and their reflections on those workings, while a grimoire is a reference book of magical items and terms. Although these are technically two different things, in recent years the terms have become interchangeable.

Full transparency here: Something I wish I'd done earlier in my practice is journaling. Although I've written down bits and pieces of my craft over the years, I didn't begin a frequent journaling habit until eight years ago. I now have a number of magical journals (I lost count to be honest), but I've made journaling part of my morning ritual and write in one particular journal every single day. In it I record the date, moon phase, divination (card pull) for the day ahead, spiritual reflection from the day before, and thoughts on my practice in general. A few times a year, I look back on my journals from years past and reflect on how my practice has changed over time and discover areas I need to work on.

Studies show it takes an average of fifty-nine to seventy days for a habit to form, and since journaling about our magical practice is key to maintaining a practice, it makes sense to integrate this into your practice right away.

Benefits of Magical Journaling

✳ MEASURES GROWTH IN YOUR PRACTICE: It's nice to see how your practice ebbs and flows over time and journaling allows you to see how you've progressed in your spiritual journey. I love looking back on my magical journals to see how much I've grown.

✳ PROVIDES ANOTHER WAY OF MEDITATING: Journaling can serve as a mindful meditation of sorts. The act of putting pen to paper—feeling the pen in your hand and its movement across the paper—is a mindful activity; prompts serve as guided meditations.

✳ OFFERS AN OUTLET FOR STRESS: Days where I'm extra frustrated or anxious about something, I turn to my journal to vent. When something in my practice doesn't make sense or I'm frustrated over an incomplete or ineffective card reading or ritual, I reflect on it and note how I can improve upon it next time.

✳ ENCOURAGES A CREATIVITY BOOST: Magical journaling and free writing about my practice often inspires me to create more magic, write out rhymes, and test out spells. As an author of fiction, journaling about my practice on a daily basis forces me to keep my writing skills intact too.

✳ KEEPS YOU CONNECTED TO YOUR PRACTICE: You can journal anytime anywhere for a quick burst of magic. It's easy to keep a small journal in your purse or pocket or a digital one on your phone when magical inspiration strikes.

Sitting in front of my altar with a hot cup of tea or an extra-hot cappuccino while writing in my journal is one of the coziest parts of my day.

Just Get Started

Many people get hung up on making their journal look pretty and are too afraid to write anything in case they "mess up." I'm here to tell you to throw that notion out the window. You are going to see elaborate Books of Shadows and creative junk journaling–style grimoires when you scroll social media, but don't let those deter you from starting your own. All you need is a notebook and a writing utensil. My magical journals are filled with mistakes, typos, spells that didn't work, inkblots, coffee stains, and the occasional bit of dog slobber (thanks, Ries and River!). Grab that gorgeous journal you picked up at Barnes & Noble two years ago and finally use it. Start writing now or you'll never start writing at all.

COLORS FOR REFLECTION: white, light blue, gray, cream, and light green
CRYSTALS FOR REFLECTION: moonstone, amazonite, clear quartz, and
  aquamarine

INNER MAGIC

Magical Journaling Exercise

Find five to ten minutes every single day for the next five days to sit in quiet journaling. Light a candle, burn your favorite incense, and open your magical journal. Free write any thoughts that come to mind about your spiritual journey and practice. Use any or all of the below guided questions if you're struggling with where to start.

GUIDED QUESTIONS

Why have I hesitated to journal in the past?

How can I benefit from magical journaling?

How can I incorporate magical journaling into my daily routine?

What tenets help define my practice? What do they mean to me?

When I think of a witchcraft practice, what comes to mind?

Who inspires me to create a magical life?

What would an ideal magical practice look like for me?

Journaling Tools

Although you by no means need any tools other than a writing utensil and some paper to do your magical journaling, I wanted to share with you some tools that may enhance your magical journaling practice. Take some time to explore some of these tools and think about adding one or two to your journal routine.

✴ WASHI TAPE: This removable tape comes in all sorts of sizes and patterns and adds an aesthetic pop to your journaling.

✴ EPHEMERA: These are items of collectible memorabilia, typically written or printed, that were originally expected to have only a short-term use like movie ticket stubs, postcards, old maps, book pages, and sheet music.

✴ DRIED FLOWERS AND HERBS: One of my favorite ways to adorn my grimoire is by adding pops of actual nature in the form of dried flowers and herbs.

✳ SCRAP AND VELLUM PAPER: Like washi tape, many witches like to add pops of texture and patterns to their magical journals. You can do this with paper scraps and vellum paper.

✳ STAMPS AND STICKERS: Adorn your journal pages with stickers and stamps of animals, crystals, moon phases, rune symbols, tarot cards, and more.

✳ OTHER JOURNAL-RELATED ITEMS TO EXPLORE: Additional enhancements for your journal pages could include rivet embellishments, 3D stickers, watercolors, lace, wax seals, and burlap.

⸙ LEVEL UP ⸙

Reawaken Your Magical Journaling

If you already keep a Book of Shadows, personal grimoire, or magical journal, try adding another form of magical writing to your practice. Look at the types of magical journals below and choose one that appeals to you. For the next week, write in this journal daily.

TYPES OF MAGICAL JOURNALS

✳ RITUAL/SPELL JOURNAL: A journal dedicated to tracking your spells and rituals

✳ DIVINATION JOURNAL: A journal to keep record of your divination results

✳ PLANT JOURNAL: A journal to keep track of planting cycles and plant/herb correspondences

MY FAVORITE COZY MAGICAL JOURNALING SHOPS

I love supporting small businesses and try to purchase most of my magical journaling supplies from them rather than relying on big-box stores. There is absolutely nothing wrong with purchasing your supplies from big-box stores; I just try to patronize small businesses when I can afford to.

- Archer & Olive
- CoraCreaCrafts
- Earth and Omen
- Journaling Home
- Notebook Therapy
- Paper Minty Studio
- Rongrong
- Saucy Stickers Co
- T's Stationery
- The Washi Tape Shop

✳ **KITCHEN/COOKING GRIMOIRE:** A journal to record your magical recipes

✳ **ASTROLOGY JOURNAL:** A journal to reflect on astrology's impact on your life

- ✴ QUOTE JOURNAL: A journal dedicated to inspirational witchcraft quotes

- ✴ DREAM JOURNAL: A journal to record and analyze your dreams

- ✴ CARD-PULL/TAROT JOURNAL: A journal dedicated to your daily card-pulling ritual

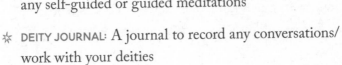

- ✴ MEDITATION REFLECTION JOURNAL: A journal to reflect on any self-guided or guided meditations

- ✴ DEITY JOURNAL: A journal to record any conversations/ work with your deities

- ✴ MAGICAL BOOK REVIEWS AND REFLECTIONS: A journal to document insights about books on magic

- ✴ SELF-CARE JOURNAL: A journal to record your self-care rituals and reflect on your mental and physical well-being

- ✴ NATURE JOURNAL: A journal to keep track of your experiences in and reflections on nature

- ✴ SPIRIT TEAM COMMUNICATION JOURNAL: A journal to record any conversations/work with members of your spirit team

- ✴ ANCESTOR JOURNAL: A journal dedicated to ancestor workings and conversations

TENET

DELIGHT

SOMETHING IMPERATIVE TO DEVELOPING A magical practice, especially a comfy cozy practice, is finding delight in the journey, and unfortunately, I think *delight* is lacking in a lot of witchcraft practices. This is the fourth tenet. When I turn to Instagram or TikTok, for example, I see a lot of serious workings, people tell others what to do and how to do it, and many memes and graphics depicting spell ingredients and correspondences and what you *should* be using, but I don't see a lot of photos and videos depicting the joy people get from their practice. Now, don't get me wrong, those more serious parts of the craft have a place and merit. And naturally, you can find a lot of great posts when looking for advice and inspiration.

What I also see is a lot of people *telling* others when and how to celebrate a sabbat, urging them to *work with the full moon while you can*, or reminding them of each moon phase, planet transit, and planet retrograde and how to embrace or avoid them, which puts a lot of pressure on you, especially if you're newer to your practice. At each sabbat, I see time and time again people rushing to celebrate in one way, shape, or form, and others have expressed to me how *guilty* they feel over not getting around to celebrating at all. Guilt and shame have no place in a magical practice. And it's important to remember that when we force something on ourselves, there comes a point where our interest, curiosity, learning, and even magic-making become a chore rather than something we look forward to.

I have to be honest, I truly enjoy every part of my practice. I look forward to sitting in my sacred space each morning and going through my daily ritual. I enjoy celebrating the sabbats with food and ritual and time spent with family. And I think a lot of that is because I choose to look at my craft from a lens of delight rather than from a lens of obligation or guilt. At one point I did feel guilty if I wasn't witchy enough or practicing enough. But once I let that feeling of guilt and obligation go, that's where the delight and authenticity of my practice shined. So now, if I don't feel like doing a ritual for the new moon, I don't do one. If I miss a sabbat celebration due to the busyness of life, I honor it some other time during that festival season, if at all. And I recommend you do the same. Your practice doesn't need to look like anyone else's. Simply find the delight in *your* magic, and you'll be well on your way to crafting a practice that is authentic to you.

COLORS FOR DELIGHT: yellow, orange, pink, red, and pastels
CRYSTALS FOR DELIGHT: citrine, pyrite, aventurine, sunstone, amethyst, rose quartz, carnelian, and fluorite

Future Journal Entry

Whether you're just starting out on your comfy cozy witchy journey or need a little refresh, you'll get a lot from completing this exercise. I'd like you to write a journal or diary entry, but date the entry one year from the day you're reading this. Write the entry with your ideal delightful, magical day in mind. Go through your day, from morning to night, detailing what it is you did to honor your spiritual journey.

Did you connect with nature and the elements by getting up early to sip on tea and listen to the birds?

Did you dedicate twenty minutes in the morning to reading a book on magic?

Did you do some kitchen witchery at dinnertime and prepare a meal with intentional ingredients?

Did you finish the day with a gratitude practice and evening ritual that nourishes your body?

When you're finished detailing your day, make a note in your journal or phone to come back to the entry one year from now to reflect on how your entry has come to fruition.

Finding Joy in Community

Sometimes we can find even more delight in our practice when we share it with others. I challenge you to find other magical people in your area—people who are starting out on their own spiritual journey, those who want to find connection with like-minded people, or those who need a renewal in a more established practice. Head to your local metaphysical shop, crystal store, or New Age business, and ask if there are any local groups you can join. If you'd rather do your research online, turn to Facebook or Meetup groups to find a local magical, spiritual, witchy, or pagan group—whatever search terms you're comfortable with. If you aren't comfortable meeting other magical people in person, interact with them on an online platform. Prompt your new friends to share what brings them delight in their magical practice. We have so much to learn from one another. Keep a list of local shops, organizations, meetups, and festivals you find. Attend one if you so choose! Journal about how this experience connecting with others went.

New Magical Experiences Challenge

Experienced practitioners can sometimes get a little stuck and set in their ways. When this happens, our practice becomes stagnant and we don't look forward to making magic anymore. When you find yourself experiencing this, I challenge you to step outside your comfort zone and attempt a new magical experience. Have you always been interested in mediumship but never took the plunge to attend a séance or take a course on it? Now's the time to do it. If there's a local pagan con or witchy conference or holistic fair nearby, go out and visit it. Introduce yourself to other attendees. Ask them about their practices and what they do to get out of a funk.

Respond to the following prompts:

Where in my practice am I lacking joy?

What can I do to step out my comfort zone to connect with others like me?

What magical experiences have I been wanting to try but haven't tried yet?

TENET

WARMTH

ONE OF THE MAIN COMPONENTS of a comfy cozy practice is warmth, tenet number five. Not only do I try to keep my house warm and inviting, but I keep my sacred space somewhere I want to come back to each and every day. My sacred space is filled with candles, a plush rug, throw blankets, meditation cushions, and general décor that evokes a feeling of ease and warmth as soon as I walk in. When I spend time in that space, I either light a candle or some incense, which over time has left a permanent scent in the room—a warm, inviting scent. Before going into that sacred space, I also brew my morning cup of coffee and stir cinnamon into it while speaking words to invite warmth into my day.

Beyond incorporating tangible warmth into our sacred spaces, I want to talk about things we can do in our practice that promote that feeling. Practicing gratitude is a way to bring warmth to our magical practice from the inside out, and I've found it to be a game changer to our spiritual lives too. I write down three things I'm grateful for every morning as part of my morning ritual. This not only helps me mindfully focus on the present, but it also allows me to find warmth and meaning beyond myself. Rarely do I express gratitude about a part of me, rather I express gratitude for other people and situations and what appeals to my senses. This practice helps us be more mindful of what is going on around us, makes us aware of the little things in life—the way the coffee steam whirls perfect spirals, the very first blossoms of spring, or a ray of moonlight illuminating the garden—and allows us to slow down for a beat. It's in those slow moments where we get glimpses of our innate magic.

COLORS FOR WARMTH: red, orange, yellow, and purple
CRYSTALS FOR WARMTH: citrine, yellow calcite, red jasper, lepidolite, amethyst, fire quartz, sunstone, and carnelian

⟩⟩⟩ INNER MAGIC ⟨⟨⟨
Gratitude Journal

You might already be familiar with the practice of writing down three things you're grateful for each day. I challenge you to not only adopt this practice for yourself but to go beyond writing the same three things every day. You can choose to write your gratitude entry each morning or evening. My mind works best in the morning, so I write about my gratitude from the day before. If you choose to complete your journal entry at night, you can jot down three things from that day that meant something good to you. No matter when you choose, know that this practice will have you reflecting on your day and being mindful of the small, magical moments and of the gifts, graces, and positive interactions you had with others.

Prompts to get you started:

Choose a positive interaction you had with someone during the day and write about it.

Turn to your senses. What smell are you grateful for . . . the scent of fresh rain on newly mowed grass? What have you heard today that makes you grateful? What have you seen?

—⟫⟫⟫ OUTER MAGIC ⟪⟪⟪—

Building a Warm, Cozy Space for Your Practice

For this outer-magic exercise, I want you to begin building a warm and cozy sacred space you can come back to when you need to connect to your spiritual, witchy self. Start by choosing a space that makes you feel *at home*. I know you may be in a small apartment or even share a room with someone else. No matter where you live or the amount of space you're working with, it's possible to carve out a small sacred space. This space may be the corner of a room where you set up a small table (your altar), a candle, a few crystals, and a deck of cards. Or maybe you're curating a sacred space that is an entire room. When you envision that space, what do you see? Do you see plants and herbs of all kinds? Do you see plush blankets and crystals? Do you see a small table with a vase of seasonal flowers and a magical journal?

And if you aren't at a place where you can begin building the space, you can plan it out. Grab a blank piece of paper and writing utensil and sketch out what your ideal sacred space looks like. We'll be doing more work with our sacred and altar spaces in chapter 8!

-·🕸 LEVEL UP 🕸·-

Compassion Cookie Recipe

Sometimes when we've practiced magic for such a long time we can be hard on ourselves when our spell work doesn't go as expected. In order to move forward with our practice, it's important we have self-compassion and give ourselves grace. Follow the recipe below to make some self-compassion cookies. Nibble on these cookies throughout the week while you complete your morning-ritual work, sip on your morning tea or coffee, journal about your divination of the day, or reflect on your most recent magical workings. Reflect on how you can show yourself more compassion and grace and how that will benefit your practice. And don't feel guilty for taking these quiet pockets of time for yourself. You deserve it!

INGREDIENTS

1½ cups sugar, plus 2 tablespoons for rolling
1 cup salted butter, softened
1 egg
2 teaspoons vanilla extract

2½ cups all-purpose flour

½ teaspoon baking soda

1 tablespoon ground cinnamon,
plus 2 teaspoons for rolling

¼ teaspoon ground nutmeg

¼ teaspoon ground cloves

Ingredients that represent compassion are cinnamon, cloves, and ginger. When you mix those into a bowl, make sure you're adding them with the intention of compassion and grace for yourself and whomever you serve the cookies to.

METHOD

1. Preheat the oven to 350°F. Line a baking sheet with parchment paper and set it aside.

2. In a large bowl, beat the sugar, butter, egg, and vanilla together until light and fluffy. Add the flour, baking soda, cinnamon, nutmeg, and cloves, and stir until combined.

3. In a small bowl, stir together 2 tablespoons sugar and 2 teaspoons cinnamon. Scoop the dough into 2 tablespoon-size balls and roll in the cinnamon-sugar mixture. Place the balls on the prepared baking sheet, leaving room for spreading.

4. Place the baking sheet in the oven and bake for 10 to 12 minutes or until the edges of the cookies are golden. Allow to cool slightly before moving the cookies to a wire rack to finish cooling completely.

TENET

BALANCE

WHEN IT COMES TO LIVING a magical life, balance is key. After all, balance is found in all things. We find it in nature with the changing of the seasons, the turning of the wheel, and the rising sun and moon, and we also find that balance within ourselves. When starting a magical practice or wanting to reinvigorate an existing one, finding the balance among our physical, emotional, and spiritual selves helps us become better practitioners, which is why it is our sixth tenet. Taking the time to check in with your emotions and understand your inner magic, nourishing your physical self, and creating a practice that honors your spiritual self is just as important as the actual doing of the magic.

And when I talk about balance, I don't mean we need to devote equal amounts of time to everything. Balance is about finding what works for you in that moment. If you feel your spiritual practice slipping because of the stressors of work, maybe devote ten minutes each morning to establishing a way to connect to your spiritual self. If you can't seem to connect with your partner or children, it could be time to put that phone down and plan some quality time together. If you've been making not-so-great eating decisions and it's taking a toll on your health, make the conscious decision to eat more foods that come from the earth—fruits, vegetables, and grains. It's amazing how a re-centering of diet and priorities can help us find balance.

When I think about balance, I always come back to self-care. When an area of my life or my being is out of balance, typically I find my self-care routine lacking. When we don't take care of ourselves, it's virtually impossible to take care of the important people and animals in our lives, which throws everything off balance. Not only is estab-lishing self-care routines and practices good for our physical selves, it's indispensable for our emotional and spiritual selves as well.

COLORS FOR BALANCE: green and blue

CRYSTALS FOR BALANCE: hematite, green aventurine, blue apatite, lepidolite, and tiger's-eye

INNER MAGIC

Self-Care Journaling Prompts

You already know by now that daily journaling and reflection is an important part of my practice. In fact, as we continue through this book, you'll find me asking you to journal and answer prompts over and over again. But it's because I've found journaling to be such a transformative part of my practice. I love looking back at old journals to see how far I've come in my magical journey. Honestly answer the following questions in the space provided or in the journal of your choice.

What does a balanced life look like to me?

In what areas of my magical practice do I feel off-balance?

What are three small self-care practices I can integrate into every day?

⟨⟨⟨ OUTER MAGIC ⟩⟩⟩

Self-Care Candle Magic

One of the simplest types of spell work is candle magic. You can do so much with a candle and an intention (something we'll go into in more depth in chapter 13). I can't say that lighting a candle will help instantly resolve every insecurity, negative self-belief, or spiritual issue you have. But it's definitely a start! This is a wonderful bit of magic to get in tune with your self-care needs.

WHAT YOU'LL NEED

Pink or white candle

2 drops ylang-ylang essential oil

2 drops rose essential oil (or any essential oil you have on hand!)

Jojoba or almond oil

Candle-safe dish or holder

Lighter or matches

METHOD

1. Take the candle and anoint it with the ylang-ylang and rose
   essential oils. (You can do this by mixing the essential oils with
   a carrier oil such as jojoba or almond oil, then rubbing the oil
   mixture on the candle.)
2. Hold the anointed candle in both hands, close your eyes, and
   charge the candle with the energy of self-care by saying, "I
   empower this candle with self-care and balance."
3. When you're in need of some balance in your life, place your
   candle on a candle-safe dish and light it. While lighting it, say, "I
   light this candle to remind me to find balance in my life."
4. Place the candle in a space in your home where you feel calm,
   safe, and relaxed. Light it as often as you can to remind yourself
   of the intention of self-care and promise of balance you have set.
   You can move it to your mirror for affirmations, light it when you
   meditate, or take a self-care bath lit by its warm flame.

⚛ LEVEL UP ⚛

Tarot Card Spread for Balance

Sometimes, as more experienced practitioners, we have a tendency
to get complacent in our practice and need a little check-in with our
favorite tarot- or oracle-card deck. Although a three-card spread
may feel a little elementary, sometimes going back to the basics is
the nudge we need to move forward. Here is a three-card spread to

help connect with your guides to assist with balance. After shuffling the deck as you see fit, choose three cards and place them side by side. Do this for five days in a row, reflecting on each spread. At the end of the five days, notice any patterns in your spreads to help pinpoint where in your life balance needs to be addressed.

Where in my life am I not putting enough energy?

Where in my life am I putting too much energy?

What would a more balanced life look like?

TENET

INTUITION

WHEN BEGINNING A SPIRITUAL JOURNEY or growing a practice, a word you're likely to encounter many times over is *intuition*. While there are many that believe intuition is a gift belonging to a selection of chosen people, intuition is a natural-born ability that each and every one of us possesses but many never use. Have you ever experienced déjà vu? Have you ever heard or smelled or just knew things no one else does? Have you ever heard a whispering in your ear or had a gut feeling something is about to go wrong and then it does? Oftentimes we chalk up instances like these when our intuition is at work as coincidences. The main ways our intuition presents itself to us are through the clair senses, also known as psychic senses. There are a handful of ways to access these clair senses, and I want to introduce you to the main five. As you read through the next few sections for this tenet, ask yourself if you've ever experienced any of the intuitive hits mentioned.

Clairvoyance

Coming from the French words *clair* and *voyance*, meaning clear seeing, clairvoyance is the ability to see through your normal sense of sight and connect to your sixth sense. Signs of clairvoyance include: having visions about the future that come true, vivid dreams that feel real, the ability to see things before they happen, the ability to tell if someone is unhealthy or struggling by looking at them, and a feel for a person's disposition upon first meeting them.

Clairaudience

From the French words *clair* and *audience*, clairaudience is the ability to receive information through hearing. A person adept in clairaudience will hear messages from their spirit guides, passed loved ones, or guardian angels. You can also hear information from your own internal dialogue or voice. Many mediums have this ability which allows them to communicate with those on the other side. Some signs that clairaudience is a strength are: you are sensitive to sounds around you, you hear sounds and voices that others don't hear, you are an auditory learner, you have conversations with yourself in your head, and you receive messages or ideas in your head as if you're being spoken to aloud.

Clairsentience

Stemming from the French words *clair* and *sentience*, meaning clear feeling, clairsentience is the ability to pick up on impressions, feelings, and emotions about people and places. This is one of the first senses we develop as children, and many of us are attuned to this sense, especially those who are empathic. When you hear the term *gut feeling*, this is the most common form of clairsentience. Signs you're in touch with clairsentience are: getting strong feelings in your stomach area when something isn't quite right, knowing the energy of a person upon first meeting them, feeling the hairs on the back of your neck stand up or goosebumps arise on your arms when encountering an uncomfortable situation, or feeling a soft touch to your head or face when thinking of a passed loved one.

Clairalience

Also known as *clairolfaction*, clairalience means clear smelling and describes the ability to detect and oftentimes identify odors that have no physical source. An often overlooked clair sense, clairalience is a clair sense that I've worked with since childhood. Because your sense of smell has the power to evoke powerful memories, messages that come to us this way are often channeled through a passed loved one. Signs you may be more willing to work with your clairalience is smelling odors nobody else can smell, being sensitive to candles and incense and scents of all kinds, and smelling vivid scents of loved ones—the perfume your grandmother wore or the cigars your great-uncle smoked and the like. This is a particularly strong clair sense of mine. I have been known to walk into a shop, someone's home, or another location and could tell something was off by an overwhelming scent only I could smell.

Clairgustance

Clairgustance, known as clear tasting, is another of the more obscure clair senses, but it doesn't make it any less important. Clairgustance is the ability to receive messages through the sense of taste. Because it's closely linked to clairalience, and our nose and mouth are connected, many people share both clairalience and clairgustance abilities. This clairgustance is most pronounced if you ever read cards for yourself or others. During a reading or interaction with another, you may get a hint of a taste that reminds you of a person, an experience, or a memory.

One of the best ways to strengthen your intuition and tap into these clair senses is to learn how to still yourself enough to recognize when you have an intuitive hit. You can still your mind through meditation or doing a body scan. You can slow your body by spending time outside, going on a mindful walk where you notice the colors, sights, smells, and other scents. You can disconnect from the noisiness of technology and social media and journal, draw, or doodle. See what comes to you as you do so. And you can even sit in a quiet space and ask your intuition a question and see what responses come to you.

COLORS FOR INTUITION: white, lilac, lavender, deep purple, and deep blue

CRYSTALS FOR INTUITION: moonstone, amethyst, lapis lazuli, selenite, and clear quartz

Intuition Stone Exercise

What you'll need

Purple candle

Candle-safe dish or holder

Lighter or matches

11 small stones (ones you find out in nature
    yourself would be best)

Journal or notebook

Writing utensil

Sachet

Method

1. Find a quiet and comfortable place to sit with your candle. Place
   your candle on a candle-safe dish and light it. Allow your mind
   to wander freely as you relax. Position the stones in a shape that
   is important to you—circle, heart, star, or another symbol. Speak
   aloud the following chant three times:

   > Stones of old speak to me, through your wisdom help me
   > see. Stones of old, ancient and wise, bring intuition to my
   > eyes. Stones so strong and from the ground, show me
   > images, scents, and sound.

2. Once you've finished speaking, pick up the stones and hold
   them in your hand. Close your eyes and listen to any thoughts
   and messages that come to you in the form of symbols, shapes,
   whispers, scents, colors, and so on. When you feel you've received

all the messages, blow out the candle and journal about as much as you can remember. Repeat the spell for as many days as you'd like to help strengthen the connection to your inner knowing and intuition and to these intuition stones. Put the stones in a small sachet and carry them with you to remind you of your inner knowing.

Intuition Dream Sachet

Create the following intuitive dream sachet to enhance your intuition and psychic messages that come across while you sleep.

What you'll need

Pinch of mugwort (psychic ability)
Pinch of dried lavender (peaceful dreaming)
3 obsidian chips (protection)
1 drop mint essential oil (clarity)
Sachet or cloth and string
Journal or notebook
Writing utensil

Method

1. Place the mugwort, lavender, obsidian chips, and essential oil in a small sachet or a cloth fastened with twine or string.
2. Place the sachet under your pillow for a week and write down any dreams and your interpretations of those dreams. Record any connections or truths your dreams reveal.

Connecting with Your Guides Journey

Although you may have been able to connect with your guides throughout your journey, take some time to connect to those guides and receive any new messages they may have for you through this meditation. I do this meditation when I need either a little boost of help from my guides or when I haven't checked in with them for quite some time. This is also similar to the meditation I completed when I first met a few of my own guides!

1. Find a quite space to sit comfortably and meditate. Have a notebook and writing utensil handy to take any notes at the end of the meditation.

2. Close your eyes and take three deep breaths. Envision yourself in the middle of the forest, surrounded by trees and plants. Listen to the birds chirp and the animals scuttle through the leaves on the ferny floor below. You're slowly walking through this forested land when up ahead you see a Celtic eye, a circle made of stone with a hole in its center large enough to walk through.

3. You walk toward the eye and step through the circle. When you arrive to the other side, you're suddenly inside a small garden filled with wildflowers, bees and butterflies flittering about. There's a stone walking path that cuts through the middle of the garden and at the end of that path sits a white bench. You walk on the stone path and slowly find your way to the bench.

4. You sit down on the center of the bench and take a few deep breaths when you suddenly feel a presence next to you. You turn to see who has joined you on the bench.

5. Who is this being next to you? Take note of its presence. Study their features—their eyes, hair, clothing, shoes. Are they holding anything? This is the guide who wishes to connect with you today.

6. Take a moment to ask this guide any questions you may have. Sit in silence and simply *listen* to what they have to say. Do they have words of advice? Do they have questions for you to ask yourself? Do they offer a name? Perhaps they say nothing at all but provide a feeling of comfort, calm, and stability. Stay with this guide for as long as you'd like, soaking in their energy and listening to anything they have to share. Take notice not only of what they're saying but also of any thoughts you have or sensations you experience.

7. Once you're satisfied with this meeting, thank your guide for joining you in this sacred space today and watch as they stand up, step behind the bench, and disappear into the forest.

8. Remain seated on the bench for as long as you'd like, going over the experience you just had with your guide until you are ready to leave yourself.

9. When you're ready, stand up from the bench. Make your way down the stone path of the garden, through the stone Celtic eye, and through the forest you first came through.

10. Slowly open your eyes and write down anything you remember about this experience with your guide.

PART 2

Making Your *Own* Magic

Now that the basics and extension exercises are completed, it's time to start building a practice. In this section, I'll guide you through outlining the creation of a sacred space and a daily ritual that fits you, we'll discuss and reflect on divination tools to enhance your practice, and finally we'll get to the creation of personal correspondences and spells, rather than relying on the words and spell work of others. The creation of your *own* sacred space, daily rituals, spells, and more will empower you to build a cozy, long-lasting practice of your own. By the end, you'll have created the basis for a magical practice that is authentic to you and comfy, cozy, and witchy in nature.

PATH-MAKING

I FIND PATH-MAKING TO BE so important when creating a practice that is all your own, especially for practitioners just starting their magical journeys or for those who are coming back to their practice after years on a hiatus. In the age of social media, it's easy to get caught up in the spells, rituals, and magic of others and attempt to mimic or copy their practice. However, comfy cozy witchcraft is not about *finding* a path or *borrowing* a path laid out by others; it's about *creating* . . . about making . . . your own way and your own magic. And that truly is at the heart of a comfy cozy practice and what you'll be doing through the rest of the book.

QUESTIONS TO PONDER:

Where have I looked for witchcraft inspiration in the past?
How do I want my practice to differ from those I see displayed in
    other books and on social media?

Sacred Space

One thing I come back to in my practice is warmth; it was a tenet after all. And your sacred space is a warm, comforting area created by you where you complete parts of your magical practice—meditations, journaling, rituals, spell work, and the like. Dedicating a space to your practice is vital, especially if you're just starting on your magical journey and want to create a practice that is long-lasting. A sacred space is so much more than a room or an altar. It's where we come to connect with deity, spirit, higher self, source, and so on. It's a place of calm and comfort that immediately takes us out of our heads and into the present. A place where we can get grounded for magical work. A place to connect with ancestors and our guides. A sacred space can be your home, a room, a balcony, your garden, a windowsill, or even yourself. When I need to connect to my practice in a comfortable way, I go to one of my many sacred spaces. I've spoken about my sacred space at length on my podcast, but I want to share now some of the sacred spaces in my life and how they've been vital to my practice.

My most cherished sacred space is my home office. In fact, I rarely refer to it as an office, rather I call it my sacred space to pretty much anyone who comes in my house. When I first walk into the room, I'm greeted each and every morning by the most calming scent created by years of burning incense and scented candles during my ritual work. In fact, the first thing people say upon entering my space is, "It smells so good in here!" (Side note: I've been attempting to replicate that scent in my apothecary and so far I've been successful because my customers say the same thing when they enter my shop!) Although I have my desk and writing and work supplies in my sacred space, where the magic happens is in the front half of the room, at my altar.

ALTAR AS A SACRED SPACE

Another sacred space—my working altar—sits in the front corner of the room, positioned at an angle, and on the floor directly in front of two large windows is what I call my floor altar. My working altar contains representations of the elements, the card deck(s) I'm currently working with, any spell work I'm currently working on, and my magical journal or Book of Shadows. The small altar on my floor is dressed in seasonal décor and sabbat representations. I sit in front of either altar each morning for my daily ritual, which I'll talk about in the next chapter. Although my altar is inside my sacred room space, I find my altar to be a sacred space in and of itself. In fact, many witches consider their altars their sacred spaces, and it's important to note that your altar and what you place on it is entirely up to you. When logging into most social media platforms, we see depictions of perfectly curated altars with smoke billowing from cauldrons, thirty candles casting soft shadows over personalized altar cloths, and the like, but I want to remind you that those you see on social media are aesthetic in nature, not necessarily working altars. All you need for your altar is a small space—my friend Rowan's altar is a windowsill and my friend Melissa's is a decorative tray—whatever items are sacred to you, and an intention to dedicate the space to magical working.

CREATING YOUR SACRED SPACE

In part 1, you already envisioned a space that emanated warmth, and I want you to take that a step further in creating your sacred space. There are no hard and fast rules when it comes to setting up a sacred space. Although you may choose to decorate your space with representations of the elements, with certain deities or Pantheons in mind, or with pictures of ancestors and passed loved ones, however you choose to set up your space is entirely up to you. For this exercise I want you to find either a space in your home to dedicate as your sacred space or find a small corner, windowsill, or small tray you can dedicate as your altar space. This space should be tucked away from foot traffic and the curious glares of others if possible, but it should be easily accessible when you want to do your magical workings, meditate, or simply be. If you have children or curious pets, you could tuck this space into a closet or on a high shelf (but one that is accessible to you!). Although we ourselves can be seen as sacred spaces (which I fully believe), when creating a practice with longevity in mind, it helps to have a tangible space to do our sacred work.

You may want to place the following items in your sacred space/ altar:

* altar broom

* artwork

* bell or chime

* books

- ✳ candles
- ✳ crystals
- ✳ deity depictions
- ✳ flowers and herbs

- ✳ incense
- ✳ meditation cushion

- ✳ seasonal décor
- ✳ shells and stones
- ✳ tapestry

- ✳ throw rug

TIPS

- ✳ Keep the space clean and tidy.
- ✳ Do frequent energetic cleanses with incense smoke or ringing a bell.

- ✳ Engage with the space on a regular basis.
- ✳ Change your altar décor with the seasons.

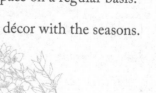

ALTAR STYLES

Although I recommend starting with one main altar at the beginning of your magical journey, I want to share a few other types of altars you may want to create over time.

- **EVERYDAY ALTAR:** This is the altar you frequent most. It may contain the items and tools you use in your practice most frequently—stones, candles, incense, divination tools, and anything else important to your practice.
- **ANCESTOR ALTAR:** This altar is a dedicated space for your passed loved ones and animals who work with you throughout your life. Common items to keep on an ancestor altar are photographs of the loved ones and offerings of their favorite items.
- **DEITY ALTAR:** A deity altar is one dedicated to the God(s)/Goddess(es) you frequently work with or wish to work with. You may include a picture or representation of that deity and any offerings that correspond with them like their sacred animal.
- **SPELL WORK ALTAR:** Also called a working altar, this altar is used for any magical practice or spell workings. It may house magical herbs, plants, oils, anointed candles, and important elemental representations, as well as your personal grimoire, Book of Shadows, or magical journals.

- **ELEMENTAL ALTAR:** If you work closely with the elements and their properties, you may wish to set up an elemental altar. I like to see these altars set up in the elements—outside. Include representations of each element:
  - **EARTH:** pentacle, stones, crystals, salt, acorns, leaves, and seeds
  - **AIR:** wand, bell, incense, herbs, and fairy representations
  - **FIRE:** wand, candle, fire crystals, sun images, and incense
  - **WATER:** shells, chalice, driftwood, water crystals, ocean images, and scrying ball

Sacred Space Dedication Ritual

Now that you've set up your altar/sacred space, you're ready to consecrate your space and dedicate yourself to working with it. Set aside twenty to thirty minutes during a time you know you won't be disturbed. The best time to perform this ritual would be at dawn, a time associated with new beginnings; however, any time in the morning or early afternoon would work. Keep in mind, like all rituals and exercises in this book, this can be adjusted and customized as you see fit.

WHAT YOU'LL NEED

Cushion or blanket (optional)

White candle

Candle-safe dish or holder

5 crystals or stones of your choice

Lighter or matches

Small dish

METHOD

1. Get comfortable in your sacred space or in front of your altar.
   Feel free to grab a cushion to sit on, a blanket to drape across
   your shoulders, or anything to make you feel safe and secure.

2. Place your candle on a candle-safe dish in the middle of your
   space and surround the candle with your five crystals, placed
   equidistant apart.

3. Light the candle with the lighter or matches, then close your eyes.
   Take three deep breaths. With each inhale envision a vibrant
   white or pale lavender light filling up your sacred space. On each
   exhale watch the light spread out across your space.

4. Open your eyes and hold your hands in front of you, palms face
   down. With conviction and intention say, "I use this sacred space
   to connect to my innate magic. May I retreat here to do magical
   workings, to meditate on my journey, and to connect with my
   guides of my highest good."

5. Now spread your hands farther apart, palms facing up this time,
   and repeat the same words again. "I use this sacred space to
   connect to my innate magic. May I retreat here to do magical

workings, to meditate on my journey, and to connect with my guides of my highest good."

6. Now place both hands over your heart and say once more, "I use this sacred space to connect to my innate magic. May I retreat here to do magical workings, to meditate on my journey, and to connect with my guides of my highest good. Be it so."

7. Close your eyes once again and continue to envision that vibrant white or pale lavender light surround you and your sacred space. Watch the light pulse with each exhale, the light growing brighter and reaching wider with each breath. Continue this breathwork for twenty-one more breaths. On the final exhale the light should encapsulate your entire room or even home.

8. Open your eyes and say, "I bring this light of protection to each magical working in this new space."

9. Close your eyes once more and breathe in and out five times. With each breath envision that light now growing smaller and smaller until all its power is in one small spot in the middle of your sacred space. Say, "May this space be blessed with magic, power, and warmth."

10. Open your eyes this final time and say a quick thank you to whomever you choose—your guides, spirit, God, a deity, and so on.

11. Sit in stillness until you are ready to close. Blow out the candle and place the stones in a small dish to the side of your sacred space, there as a reminder of the sacred ritual you just performed.

12. Come back to this consecrated space for all your intention setting, meditations, journaling, and magical endeavors.

DAILY RITUAL

WHEN STARTING A MAGICAL PRACTICE or reinvigorating one you've already established, it's important to set up a daily ritual that keeps you connected to your magic in some way, shape, or form. I want to take a moment, though, to discuss the difference between ritual and routine. When we think of a routine, it's something we do on a regular basis almost on autopilot. We wake up in the morning, check our phones, brush our teeth, make coffee and breakfast, get ready for the day, and head to work—that is a routine. In fact, we don't give much thought at all to our daily routine. However, a ritual is something done on a consistent basis that is mindful in nature, rather than completed on autopilot. A daily ritual is done with *intention*. It is cozy in nature, nourishment for our spiritual selves, and a reminder of the magic that surrounds us everywhere.

If you've listened to my podcast, you know I've spoken at length about my daily rituals; however, the episode dedicated to daily rituals was released four years ago, so naturally my daily ritual has changed over time. I want to share with you my current daily ritual. Perhaps it will give you some ideas and ways to create a doable daily ritual of your own.

Since opening my brick-and-mortar Comfy Cozy Apothecary, I sleep in a bit later than I used to. Now, when I sleep in, I'm talking 6:30 . . . nothing too drastic. After getting out of bed and doing my morning *routine*, I then make my way to the kitchen where my morning *ritual* begins. First, I make a cup of coffee. I like to do this when all is quiet in the house, before the morning chaos that consists of the get-ready-for-school routine, the let-out-and-feed-the-dogs routine, and more.

I intentionally stir a teaspoon of honey into my coffee, asking it to sweeten my day. Then I stir in a pinch of cinnamon for protection and warmth. While I do this, I ask my guides to join me for my day by simply saying, *"Guides and ancestors of my highest good, I invite you to join me for my day."* I then make my way into my sacred space, which is my office, and take a seat at my altar situated in the corner. I'll be sure to grab some crystals, whatever oracle or tarot deck I wish to work with, and my magical journal before I sit down. I like to light a candle while I sit at my altar, and most days I also light my favorite incense—Nitiraj or Nag Champa. After closing my eyes for a few minutes of meditation and deep breathing, I open my journal and write down the date, moon phase, three things I'm grateful for, and anything of note that came to my mind while meditating. I then pull a card (or cards) for the day, reflect on that for a bit, and journal about it.

My daily ritual can take anywhere between five minutes and

upward of an hour to complete, and I don't feel like myself when I neglect to take that sacred time for myself in the morning. My cozy morning ritual sets the tone for my day, reminding me of my innate magic and of the magic in the small things.

Even if I'm not able to sit down and do my typical daily ritual, I like to *touch* my magic in some way, shape, or form on a daily basis. That could mean pulling a card without jotting down its meaning to me. It could come in the form of a five-minute morning meditation I listen to on my Insight Timer app. It could even be simply reading through past entries in my magical journal. Whatever it is, it is a way to touch or connect with my practice in the simplest of ways. Remember—your practice does not need to be something elaborate or drawn-out to make it worthwhile. Don't let anyone tell you otherwise. It simply has to fit somewhere in your life. It's through these small, meaningful rituals that the magic is made.

Making Daily Happenings a Ritual

Let's start simply by adding ritual to more mundane tasks. Below are some ways to ritualize otherwise mundane and routine tasks. Choose three or four of these tasks to ritualize over the next few days.

* **RITUALIZE YOUR SHOWER.** While you wash your hair or rub soap on your body, envision all negative energies leaving your body and washing down the drain.

✳ RITUALIZE CLEANING. Dusting and vacuuming can be quite the mundane, boring task, but add a touch of intention while you do it. Like a ritual shower, as you clean, envision stagnant energy being swept, mopped, and dusted away.

✳ RITUALIZE CREATIVITY. Construct a vision board for how you want your home to look and/or plan out where you want to add pops of magic into your home. Think of the intention you're trying to set for your home as you create your board.

✳ RITUALIZE EATING. Rather than eating out of routine—inhaling your food and drinks—take time to really savor every bite and sip. Slowly chew your food, tasting all the unique flavors and ingredients. Be mindful of the food's smell, taste, texture, and even the sound of it when you chew.

✳ RITUALIZE WALKING. Instead of the same routine of walking the dogs or walking around the neighborhood or local park, do a mindful walk where you pay attention, on purpose, to all the sights and smells in your environment.

✳ RITUALIZE COOKING. While you're preparing a meal, rather than going through the motions of following a recipe, connect with each ingredient by saying its name aloud and how it can nourish your body and family. Thank the food for giving you sustenance.

✳ RITUALIZE GARDENING. Rather than mindlessly planting your herbs and flowers or tending to your plants, do a quick search on the best moon phase to plant and harvest crops.

CREATING A RITUAL THAT FITS *YOU*

A great way to connect with yourself, to deepen your intuition, and to quiet your mind is through setting up a daily ritual—one that you complete on a daily (or if not daily, a regular) basis. You've already created and consecrated a sacred space, so the next logical step is to use that space as part of your magical practice. In this exercise, you'll create a ritual that fits you and your schedule. Think about the best time to perform your daily ritual. If you have more time and energy in the morning, then create a ritual to perform then. If you're a night owl and get a boost of energy in the evening when all is quiet in the house, choose that as your ritual time. Then think about what you want to include in your ritual. A meditation? A divination of some sort (see the next chapter for more!)? Some magical journaling? Jot down your ideas below.

Ideal time:

Setting the scene:

Ritual:

DIVINATION

THE ART OF DIVINING THE future has been practiced for thousands of years. The ancient wise men and women were fascinated with recurring patterns in nature—the flight of birds, the ripples in water, the placement of animal bones, the shapes leaves took when they fell, the placement of stones and shells, and more. Although there are many people today who believe forms of divination do, indeed, divine the future, there are many (like me) who believe that acts of divination show us a way to understand and accept the possibilities within ourselves in the *present* moment.

I've been using divination tools for years, and my go-to form is through my oracle and tarot cards. I've accrued more than fifty decks over the years (an almost embarrassing number!). I also work with pendulums on a regular basis. I have a number of friends who use the Celtic Ogham divination tool and my friend Lane uses his goldfish as a divination tool. You heard that right! He has a fishpond in his backyard and part of his morning ritual is going outside to visit his fan-tailed friends. If they're swimming around in happy little patterns, this indicates he'll have an auspicious day. If they are moving slowly or even nipping at one another, this tells him he needs to tread carefully for the day. There are endless kinds of divinatory tools, but I want to chat about the most common ones.

Divination Tools

Although we can divine with the use of truly anything we get our hands on, when just starting a magical practice, it's nice to understand some of the more common divination tools. These tools connect us to our guides and our intuition to assist in decision-making and give guidance. They are forms of communicating with our deities, energy, and higher selves, and they help us to seek information and guidance or to receive messages.

Note: When using divination tools, it's important to protect yourself and your energy. You can perform a grounding ritual where you envision a sphere of protection around you, you can use a cleansing spray made with a variety of essential oils and herbs, you can burn incense or herbs, or you can cast a circle of protection. Whichever you decide to do, make sure you go into any divination exercise grounded and with an intention in mind.

✳ TAROT: It's thought that tarot has been around since the Middle Ages as a form of connecting to intuition and predicting the future. The cards, broken down into the major and minor arcanas, depict the fool's journey, a representation of the stages in life and aspects of ourselves. We'll be looking closer at the tarot in chapter 14.

✳ PENDULUM: A pendulum is used to connect to our higher selves/intuition/spirit team, to guide us on yes or no questions. Made of crystals and suspended from a chain, this divination tool can be carried and used anywhere. The way in which the pendulum swings after asking a question will give you an answer. Many use a pendulum board when divining this way, while others assign a swinging direction to answers.

✳ RUNES: The rune—meaning secret or hidden—is a twenty-four-alphabetic symbology that connects to a higher power or intuition to give guidance. You can close your eyes and choose a rune from a pouch to "hear" your message, toss them gently from the bag and see where they land to decode a message, or you can do an elaborate grid reading with them. We'll also be looking closer at runes in chapter 14.

✳ TASSEOMANCY: Tasseomancy or tasseography is a divination method that interprets symbols, patterns, and formations in tea leaves, coffee grounds, or wine sediment for guidance. Simply sip on a loose-leaf/coffee-ground/sedimentary beverage. When you have just a sip left, turn your cup over on a saucer or plate. Flip the cup with the opening toward you and peer inside it. See what intuitive hits come from the position of the leaves or grounds.

✳ SCRYING: Stemming from the root word *descry*, meaning to reveal, scrying is a method of divination that gives guidance by peering into an object such as a crystal ball, glass, mirror, candle flame, or incense smoke. As images and shapes take form in whatever medium is used, you can interpret the meaning by listening to your intuition.

✳ ORACLE CARDS: Like the tarot, oracle cards are used to give
guidance on a question, or a particular topic or situation,
or simply to provide guidance for the day. Unlike the tarot,
however, oracle decks vary in subject, card amount, and artwork.
I like to pull an oracle card each morning to serve as guidance
for my day, and I like to reflect on that particular card and its
relevance to my day before bed each evening.

Bibliomancy Exercise

A basic and straightforward method of divination is through
bibliomancy. Bibliomancy—*biblio*, meaning book, and *mancy*,
meaning divining—is the art of using a book as an oracle of sorts.
This is a fun way of divination that relies on your intuition with
answers between the pages of a book.

WHAT YOU'LL NEED

Favorite book (many people use something like the works of
   Shakespeare, poems of Edgar Allan Poe or Emily Dickinson, or
   even the Bible)
Writing utensil
Journal or notebook

METHOD

1. Find a quiet place (your sacred space, perhaps?) and make yourself comfortable.
2. Take a few deep breaths to ground and center yourself then grab the book of your choice.
3. Close your eyes and leaf through the pages of the book with the tips of your fingers. As you do this, think of a simple question like, *What do I need to know today?* or *Who do I need to connect with today?* or *Who am I today?*
4. Continue flipping through the pages and when you're called to stop on a certain page, do just that. Without looking, run your fingers over the pages the book is open to. When you're called to stop, then do it. Perhaps your fingers tingle or your hand gets warm. Or maybe you have an inner knowing of when it's time to stop. Just know wherever you stopped is where you were meant to.
5. Open your eyes and read the word, phrase, or sentence where your finger is pointing. Write this down in your journal and begin to brainstorm and intuitively write what it could possibly mean. Feel free to use the glossary in the back of this book for common symbols and their meanings for help.
6. Throughout the day, refer back to the words, phrase, or sentence and see how it may have relevance to your current situation or if/how it answers the question you had in mind when you started the divination.

Divination in Your Magical Journal

Many magic practitioners choose to dedicate a journal or section of their magical journals to divination. When I was starting my practice years ago, I had a separate notebook just for divination study and practice. In it, I'd write down any predictions I had, dreams, and ghost stories I'd write. Okay, so maybe it wasn't entirely dedicated to divination, but you get the point. My most recent divination journal contains notes from a tarot course I took and my experiences with the course and discoveries.

I challenge you to either start a section in your magical journal or dedicate an entire journal to your divinations. Write down notes you take from books, daily oracle- or tarot-card pulls, and your experiences with new divination methods. Make sure you come back to this journal and reread past divinations. They may reveal some interesting connections.

⚞ LEVEL UP ⚟

Try a New Divination Method

I don't know about you, but sometimes I get a bit bored with the same divination method. I pull cards every day, which is a part of my daily ritual, but sometimes I crave a new form of divination. Over the years, I've worked with runes, had my palm read, performed crystal ball and candle scrying, and even have had great experiences with my scrying mirror. Each time I switch up my divination method I feel it gives my practice a boost of new excitement. I challenge you to choose a divination method that is either unfamiliar to you or one you've only worked with a handful of times. Dedicate an evening to learning about that method and then practice it the best you can.

Divination method:

Time of day:

Materials needed:

Notes and outcome:

INTENTIONAL MAGIC

WHATEVER YOU CALL IT—INTENTIONAL MAGIC, manifestation, or spell work—at the heart of every magical working is a reason or intention. In this chapter I'll be touching upon a variety of intentions, their common correspondences, and short and sweet intention-based rituals for you to try. All the rituals in this chapter are intentionally based, easy to complete with limited time and resources, and a great way to instill a touch of magic in your daily life. When beginning a magical practice or trying to reconnect to one, simplicity often does the trick. Simplicity is one of the tenets of my comfy cozy practice, after all.

For each intention, I've also included a longer spell for you to try if you'd like. I always say *practice makes magic*, so take some of the shorter spells and rituals throughout this chapter, adapt them as you see fit, and apply them to your life. Our practices won't get stronger if we neglect to do any sort of magic.

Magic for Protection

Protection magic is some of the oldest and most practiced type of spell work. For thousands of years, dating back to the ancient Egyptians, Greeks, and Romans, protection workings have been performed to protect family members, homes, property, and animals, and to ward against hexes and curses. Today protection magic is done to clear away stagnant energy, shield you from any negative energy, and to strengthen your own protective barrier. It's also used to preserve energy and to repel people who have bad intentions.

PROTECTION CORRESPONDENCES

CRYSTALS: black tourmaline, jet, onyx, obsidian, quartz, and howlite

HERBS: angelica, basil, black pepper, clove, rosemary, geranium, sage, frankincense, cedarwood, lavender, clover, and anise

COLORS: black, deep blue or purple, and white

ANIMALS: wolves and dragons

SYMBOLS: iron nails, rope and chain, rowan's cross, and arrows

SMALL RITUALS FOR PROTECTION

✳ Plant herbs with protective properties around your home. If you're unable to plant outside or don't have an outdoor space, bring potted plants and herbs inside. Not only will they energetically protect your home, but they'll also add a soothing element to your space.

✳ Wear a bracelet made from red thread. The use of red thread is a commonly practiced folk tradition that helps ward off the "evil eye" and negativity. Tie nine knots in the thread beforehand for an added boost of protection and then tie the string around your wrist.

✳ Recite a prayer of protection to the elements, your guides, angels, spirit, and so on. This invites protective energy into your day. It can be as simple or as elaborate as you'd like. Use this as a guide: *Guides, angels, and the power of the elements, protect me as I go about my day, warding me from negativity.*

✳ Use smoke magic to clear away negative energy and any unwanted spirits. Smoke has long been used to oust entities and energies with ill intentions. Use a favorite incense or ethically sourced dried herbs to do this. Please use caution when burning any herbs.

✳ Clear clutter from your home to clear out old stagnant energy. Although this may seem like a mundane task, if you're doing it with the intention of clearing out old energies, then it's magical. Before bringing a new item into your space, ask yourself if its energy will serve you and your home.

✳ Burn a black or white candle with the word *protect* etched into it. One of the simplest rituals for protection is to do a touch of candle magic. Using a pin or other fine, sharp object, etch the word *protect* or a protection symbol into the candle. Light the candle and envision the negative energies leaving your space.

* Do a short protection visualization meditation. Take a few deep breaths in and out and envision a white bubble of light surrounding you. Imagine the bubble growing wider with each breath until its protective shell has encompassed the room or even the house.

* Create a mini protection altar for your car, in your office, or in a corner of your home. Bring in some of your favorite protective herbs or crystals and keep them in a safe place wherever you may need protection.

* Enchant an object to carry with you for protection. Grab your favorite piece of jewelry, a commonly worn item of clothing, or even a keychain. Holding the object in your left hand, cover the item with your right hand. Close your eyes and say, "I imbue this item with protection. Whenever I have it close, may it dispel any negative energies."

* Set an even more specific intention for protection. As you perform any of the above protection rituals, feel free to set a specific intention and say that intention aloud. For example, if you're traveling you may say, "Protect my family as we travel to the beach today." Or if you're starting a new job you may say, "Protect me from any new negative energies, seen or unseen, I may encounter in the workplace."

Protection Bathing Ritual

~~~~~~~~~~~~~~~~~~~~~~

Very much like the healing baths of ancient Rome, a ritual bath is meant to cleanse your aura, rebalance your energy, wash away energy that doesn't serve you, and leave you feeling recharged and abundant.

WHAT YOU'LL NEED

Candles and soft music (optional)
Bathtub
Protective bath salts (you can make these yourself by combining
    1 cup Epsom salts, ¼ cup sea salt, and three drops of a
    corresponding essential oil like lavender, rosemary, peppermint,
    or sweet orange)

METHOD

1. Feel free to set the tone with candles, soft music, etc. Fill your bathtub with water at the temperature of your liking.
2. Once filled, get in the bath and hold the ritual salts in your hand. Say, "These salts protect, cleanse, and revitalize me."
3. Pour the salts into the water and stir them clockwise while repeating the words above two more times.
4. Enjoy the soothing scent of your bath and indulge in the self-care ritual. While you soak, envision any and all negativity leaving your body. Clear your mind of the goings-on of the day and be present in the feel of the water and scent of the salts.

Two terms you'll hear when talking about protection are *banish* and *ward*. Although both are forms of protection magic, they do differ. Warding is a gentler form of defensive magic that is used to protect and guard from any negative energies. Warding redirects the bad energy away from you and from your space. Banishing is a bit more specific and direct, as it's used to get rid of a specific energy, entity, or person. Banishing is also a stronger form of defensive magic you want to be careful with. Here are a few ways to ward and banish.

WARD

- Wear corresponding crystals as jewelry to protect against negative energy.
- Place crystals in and around a room or home to ward against energies.
- Sprinkle herbal oils on yourself and your space as a protective barrier.
- Visualize a white bubble of protective light around you.
- Draw pentacles with water on all doors and windows in your home to ward and protect.
- Sprinkle salt around your doors and windows to serves as a barrier.

- Enchant a small object or create a protection spell bottle using corresponding herbs and stones to keep at the entrance of your home.

BANISH

- Create a banishing sigil and place it in the space you wish to banish energy from.
- Use a smoke wand made from dried herbs of your choosing to force energy from a space.
- Create a spray to spritz around your home to banish bad energy.
- Burn a sheet of paper with the name or title of what you'd like to banish.
- Use your intuition and any method that calls to you. Just do a bit of research before performing something you're uncertain about.

Magic for Abundance

Just like protection magic, abundance and prosperity magic has been performed for thousands of years. Ancient peoples would perform all sorts of spells and rituals during the growing seasons so their crops would be abundant enough to get them through the trials of winter. Today I know when many hear the word *abundance* they first think of money, but remember abundance comes in a variety of forms. Maybe you want to attract new friends. Or perhaps you're looking to partake in a new hobby. Think about what makes you feel prosperous besides financial security.

ABUNDANCE CORRESPONDENCES

CRYSTALS: citrine, aventurine, pyrite, jade, and peridot
HERBS: clary sage, sweet orange, patchouli, allspice, bay leaves, jasmine, cinnamon, bergamot, and basil
COLORS: green, yellow, and gold
ANIMALS: rabbit, car, horse, dolphin, and bull
SYMBOLS: coins or paper money, pentacle, silver, stars, dollar signs, and personal abundance sigil

SMALL RITUALS FOR ABUNDANCE AND PROSPERITY

✳ Practice gratitude regularly. A regular gratitude practice is a great way to invite in prosperity and abundance. When we're in a grateful mindset, we're more open to receiving even more.

* Create a money jar. Money jars are such a fun way to invite some prosperity into your life. Simply grab a jar that seals (a mini Mason jar will work), and add some peridot or aventurine crystal chips, a few pinches of basil or thyme, a few drops of patchouli oil, three pennies, and a dollar bill.

* Do some mantra/affirmation work. Repeat mantras and affirmations of abundance when you're in need of some prosperity. Say the mantra at least three times. Here are a few to begin with:

> *I deserve and attract abundance. I achieve whatever*
> *I set my mind to. I am grateful for the positive things*
> *in my life. I have everything I need for success. I believe*
> *in myself and my capabilities. I am capable, talented,*
> *and intelligent. It's easy and natural for me*
> *to be successful.*

* Create a crystal grid for abundance. Using stones that attract abundance and prosperity, create a crystal grid. You can do this with one clear quartz crystal surrounded by six small citrine or aventurine tumbles. Keep this in a place where you would most like to attract abundance.

* Create an abundance vision board. This creative ritual entails finding imagery that represents abundance to you and what you wish to bring into your life. Keep your vision board in a place you see regularly.

✳ Listen to a guided meditation about welcoming abundance into your life. There are many free guided meditations on the Insight Timer app (I swear they don't pay me, it's just *that* good). Go to your sacred space, light a candle or some incense, then listen.

✳ Clear out clutter to make room for abundance. Although on the more mundane end of the spectrum, clearing out the clutter mentally prepares you for abundance. Donate items that no longer serve you to your local thrift shop.

✳ Get to know abundance stones and the ones that work for you. Although I love using aventurine for abundance, that stone may not resonate with you. Grab a few stones traditionally associated with abundance. Sit in your sacred space and hold each stone to your chest asking for one connected to abundance to stand out. If you feel any sort of vibration or sense of ease overwhelm you while holding one—that is your stone for abundance.

Spell for Abundance

~~~~~~~~~~~~

WHAT YOU'LL NEED

Writing utensil

Small piece of paper

Spell bottle created by you or corresponding crystals

Green or white candle

Candle-safe dish or holder

Lighter or matches

METHOD

1. On the evening of the new or waxing moon, write your abundance intention on the small piece of paper. Be specific.
2. Place the paper underneath the spell bottle or crystals and the candle. Set the candle on a candle-safe dish, and light the candle.
3. Say, "I welcome and embrace abundance and prosperity into my life." Repeat twice more.
4. Meditate on what you wish to come to fruition until you feel satisfied.
5. Blow out the candle and keep your paper and jar or crystals on your altar, sacred space, or your person to remind you of this intention.

Magic for Love/Self-Love

I discussed the need for self-care in part 1 of the book, and I do feel its importance bears repeating. If we don't love ourselves and care for ourselves, how can we be expected to love and care for others? There is quite a bit of controversy in the witchcraft world when it comes to love spells. When I practice magic for love, it's in the form of self-love, self-compassion, and self-care rituals. I'm not a fan of trying to manipulate the will of others by performing spells that attract a particular person. However, I am not at all opposed to performing spells with the intention of attracting romantic attention. Just tread carefully.

LOVE/SELF-LOVE CORRESPONDENCES

CRYSTALS: rose quartz, amethyst, rhodonite, pink manganocalcite, green calcite, jade, and pink jade

HERBS: rose, rosehips, lavender, juniper, jasmine, cardamom, cinnamon, and honeysuckle

COLORS: pink, red, and green

ANIMALS: swans, penguins, horses, dolphins, ladybugs, and lovebirds

SYMBOLS: heart, rose, harp, clover, Aphrodite, infinity sign, key, and circle or ring

SMALL LOVE / SELF-LOVE RITUALS

✳ Keep a piece of rose quartz on your bathroom counter or on a windowsill next to your shower for help with self-love. The ultimate self-care and self-love stone, rose quartz is known to connect to the energy of beauty and self-confidence.

✳ Cook your favorite meal. Nothing screams self-care like sitting down to a home-cooked meal consisting of your favorite foods. For me, that is homemade macaroni and cheese with sweet stewed tomatoes. Draw a pentacle with your wooden spoon in whatever you're making for an added boost of magic from the elements.

✳ Take a self-love ritual bath or shower. See below for a ritual-bath spell for you to perform.

✳ Do some self-love journaling. There's truly no better way to work through your feelings and problems than writing them down. Boost this by pulling a few oracle or tarot cards to home in on what you need to move forward.

✳ Get in some mindful movement. Take some time out of your day (you only need ten minutes or so) to do some yoga and stretches.

With each pose repeat the following words aloud or in your head, *I am worthy of love and I care for myself.*

✳ Step away from the phone. Disconnecting from social media has proven time and time again to be beneficial to our mental health. Not only is it a time-suck, but we often find ourselves comparing our magical practices to the practices of others, which is not good. Put away the phone and focus on yourself and your practice.

✳ Wear jewelry made of rose quartz, rhodonite, or carnelian to attract love/self-love. Hold the jewelry in your hands, sending the intention of love to it whenever you wear it.

✳ Create a bedtime ritual. My nightly ritual consists of mixing organic lavender essential oil into my lotion and rubbing it on my body with the intention of peaceful sleep and good dreams. I then end with a card pull. Come up with a nightly routine that focuses on self-care and restful sleep.

Spell for Love/Self-Love

WHAT YOU'LL NEED

Writing utensil

Small piece of paper

Corresponding crystals, such as rose quartz or amethyst

Red, pink, or white candle

Candle-safe dish or holder

Lighter or matches

METHOD

1. Write your love/self-love intention on the paper (attracting love, new friendship, self-acceptance, and so on).
2. Place the paper underneath the crystals and candle. Set the candle on a candle-safe dish, and light the candle.
3. Say, "I welcome and embrace love and compassion into my life." Repeat twice more.
4. Meditate on what you wish to come to fruition until you feel satisfied.
5. Blow out the candle and keep your paper and crystals on your altar, sacred space, or person to remind you of this love/self-love intention.

Magic for Inspiration, Creativity, and Joy

As an author of both fictional works for children and teens and an author of nonfiction for adults, a lot of my spell work surrounds inspiration and creativity. Over the years I've performed many rituals and magical workings to help guide my creative process, and I have to say, I know those workings have had an impact on my success as an author.

One of the tenets of a comfy cozy magical practice is finding the joy and delight in our lives and in our craft. There are going to be times when we get in a slump—either with our practices or with our mundane lives. It's important to know that we can change that energy with a little help from our spiritual practice through small rituals.

CORRESPONDENCES FOR INSPIRATION AND CREATIVITY

CRYSTALS: blue apatite, lapis lazuli, carnelian, and citrine

HERBS: rosemary, eucalyptus, spearmint, peppermint, verbena, and lemongrass

COLORS: blue, orange, and yellow

ANIMALS: bees, hummingbirds, cats, lions, and butterflies

SYMBOLS: sun, moon, Awen, lightning, and rainbow

CORRESPONDENCES FOR JOY

CRYSTALS: carnelian, citrine, malachite, rose quartz, lapis lazuli, kiwi jasper, and orange calcite

HERBS: St.-John's-wort, chamomile, lavender, holy basil, saffron, lemon balm, and sunflower

COLORS: yellow, orange, pink, red, peach, and lilac

ANIMALS: bluebird, dog, squirrel, goat, monkey, dolphin, and dragonfly

SYMBOLS: sun, flower, rainbow, olive branch, lotus flower, crescent moon, hamsa, and shamrock

SMALL RITUALS FOR INSPIRATION, CREATIVITY, AND JOY

✳ Carry a citrine stone with you or wear a piece of citrine jewelry to invite joy and happiness into your life. Citrine has been referred to as "the success" stone filled with joy and sun energy to bring motivation, inspiration, and happiness to its wearer.

✳ Mix a few drops of peppermint essential oil into plain lotion for a boost of creativity. Peppermint awakens the senses and helps you see projects clearly, so it's a great oil to use in work surrounding inspiration and creativity. Inhaling the steam from a hot cup of peppermint tea does the trick as well.

✳ Spread joy by helping and working with others. Sometimes we get so stuck in our own heads and practices that we forget to reach out to others. Make a point to touch base with a magical friend and share stories of your spiritual practice . . . the good, the bad, and the ugly! It's amazing how joyful connecting with other like-minded people is.

✳ Soak in the sun's energy. One of the best ways to tap into happiness is by spending time in the sun. Step outside, close your eyes, and feel the sun's warmth wrap around you. Smile as the light shines down on you. You can't help but be happy. Take that energy with you by envisioning the rays shining into your crown and filling your entire body.

✳ Get moving! One of the best ways to boost creativity and inspiration is by getting off your chair or out of the office and taking a walk. Some of my best ideas come to me while walking the dogs in the early morning.

✳ Take a mind-clearing bath or shower. Spray your shower with a mix of eucalyptus oil, distilled water, and a few tablespoons of witch hazel. Let the steam open up the eucalyptus scent and breathe in deeply. This will clear your mind and make way for inspiration.

✳ Put on your favorite witchy tunes and dance! This may feel silly at first, but believe me, you'll be feeling joyful and inspired in no time. Sometimes we just need to tap into some of that playful childlike energy.

Elemental Spell for Creativity

This is a great spell to use when you're embarking on a new project or creative endeavor. Complete this ritual in the space where you'll be working on your project. If it's a work task, complete this at work (when you're alone, of course). If it's a new writing project, complete this at your desk. If it's a magical project, maybe you'll want to complete this spell in your sacred space or at your altar.

WHAT YOU'LL NEED

Representation for each element
  Earth: a crystal, pentacle, bowl of dirt or salt, or flower
  Water: a bowl of water, blue or aquamarine crystal, shell, or tarot
    card from the cups suit
  Fire: a candle, some incense, or an orange or a red crystal
  Air: some incense, a feather, a bird depiction, or a tarot card from
    the swords suit
Journal or notebook
Writing utensil

METHOD

1. Cleanse your space both physically and energetically before you begin.
2. Place your earth object in the direction of north in your space. You can use a compass to find north, or place it to the north in relation to your space—upper center. Call the element earth by saying, "Lend your creative power to [*whatever project you're working on*]."
3. Place your water object in the direction of west on your space. Call to this element by saying, "Lend me your flow and fluidity to [*whatever project you're working on*]."
4. Place your fire object in the direction of south in your space. Call to this element by saying, "Lend me your motivation for [*whatever project you're working on*]."
5. Finally, place your air object in the direction of east. Call to this element by saying, "Lend me your clarity and logic when moving forward on [*whatever project you're working on*]."
6. Once you've called in each element and asked for their help, take note of any shifts in your work mentality. Journal about this ritual. When you're finished, thank each element in the reverse order. Simply say, "Thank you, element of air, for sending me clarity. You're free to leave this space." Continue through each of the other elements.

Additional Rituals and Advice from Fellow Comfy Cozy Witches

I reached out to a few of my favorite comfy cozy witches to get their ideas and rituals that help them. I hope one (or more!) of these ideas helps light a spark for you.

* TEELA: Trust my intuition. It has saved my life a few times in the last year alone when my body felt wrong. Don't dismiss any feelings you have. Daily protection prayers. Refreshing offerings weekly.

* JOY: I keep black and white candles in large glass jars from the dollar store. One set in my living area near the front door and the other on my kitchen bar. I light them often to help create a barrier of sorts to keep negativity and bad intentions at the door. I also have cinnamon sticks above my front door [for protection].

* CAROLYN: I have worked some big healing and healing from trauma spells in the last year. To reinforce or refresh those spells, I find restating the mantras or intentions to be powerful and meaningful. Sometimes I do this after a calm morning ritual, before bed, or in the heat of stress. After, I feel stronger, taller, and more fierce.

* SALLY: Grief poppet, grief crystals, and meditation with proper sound frequencies to help heal grief. And journaling.

* ALLISON: I keep a rose quartz "plate" in my bathroom and set lotions on top of it [to be infused].

- **SKYE:** I sometimes draw protection sigils into my face cream just before I put it on in the morning, on days where I feel I need a bit more protection than others. I often carry a hag stone in my work bag/in my pocket, and have a couple placed around the house for protection.
- **IRENE:** I always stir a pentacle into my coffee or tea every day. I often veil, especially at work, and I keep a protection jar in my middle console of my car.
- **SARA:** Every morning while I water the rosemary on my front porch, I say, "May our troubles be less and our blessings be more, and nothing but good things come through our door." I thank the rosemary for its work in protecting the entrance to our home.
- **ALLISON:** Protection is a daily simple ritual for me. I wear a black tourmaline quartz bracelet every single day. When I put it on, I simply say, "Protect me today." I thank the bracelet when I take it off and place it on a selenite tower overnight for charging.

12

CORRESPONDENCE
CREATION EXERCISES

SO FAR WE'VE REVIEWED THE tenets that make up a comfy cozy witch-craft practice. You've completed exercises that got you thinking about your inner and outer magic. You've created a sacred space and daily ritual that best fits you and your life. You've been introduced to intentional magic and small, tangible things you can do on a daily basis to work with specific intentions, including sample spells for you to adapt to your liking. Now we're moving into the part of the book where you'll begin crafting a practice that is unique to you.

Although I've listed a number of common correspondences of protection in the glossary, those are commonly used traditional correspondences and may not be correspondences personal to you or local to you. So much of creating a powerful spell or magical writing is in the meaning the words and phrases you use have to *you*. Sure, a book, or even I, may tell you to reach for a black candle or a piece of obsidian for protection, but perhaps a deep blue candle or slab of labradorite feels more like protection to you. These next exercises and the writing space provided are where you can create your own correspondences to add to your magical workings. You'll be using your own experiences, intuition, and feelings, not those from books you've read or practitioners you've studied with, to come up with this personal correspondence list. The magic is in the power of *your* words, so make them yours!

PROTECTION CORRESPONDENCE CREATION EXERCISE

Complete the following imagery exercise to discover your own protection correspondences to use in future magical workings.

What you'll need

Journal

Writing utensil

Method

Go to your sacred space or sit in front of your altar. Make sure the area is cleansed and ground yourself. Take three deep breaths and close your eyes. Speak the word *protection* aloud over and over. As you do so, take notice of what images, animals, sounds, colors, tastes, and feelings come to you as you repeat the word *protection*. You could even say *animal for protection, color for protection, herb of protection* separately, and write down what comes to mind. As an image, sound, taste, or feeling comes to you, jot it down in the space provided below or in your magical journal.

PERSONAL PROTECTION CORRESPONDENCES

Colors:

Herbs:

Gemstones:

Sounds:

Animals:

Elements:

ABUNDANCE AND PROSPERITY
CORRESPONDENCE CREATION EXERCISE

Complete the following imagery exercise to discover your own abundance and prosperity correspondences to use in future magical workings.

What you'll need

Journal

Writing utensil

Method

Go to your sacred space or sit in front of your altar. Make sure the area is cleansed and ground yourself. Take three deep breaths and close your eyes. Speak the words *abundance and prosperity* aloud over and over. As you do so, take notice of what images, animals, sounds, colors, tastes, and feelings come to you as you repeat the words *abundance and prosperity*. You could even say *animal for abundance*, *color for prosperity*, *herb of prosperity* separately, and write down what comes to mind. As an image, sound, taste, or feeling comes to you, jot it down in the space provided below or in your magical journal.

PERSONAL ABUNDANCE AND PROSPERITY CORRESPONDENCES

Colors:

Herbs:

Gemstones:

Sounds:

Animals:

Elements:

LOVE/SELF-LOVE AND COMPASSION
CORRESPONDENCE CREATION EXERCISE
———————————

Complete the following imagery exercise to discover your love/self-love correspondences to use in future magical workings.

What you'll need

Journal

Writing utensil

Method

Go to your sacred space or sit in front of your altar. Make sure the area is cleansed and ground yourself. Take three deep breaths and close your eyes. Speak the word *love* aloud over and over. As you do so, take notice of what images, animals, sounds, colors, tastes, and feelings come to you as you repeat the word *love.* You could even say *animal for love*, *color for self-love*, *herb of compassion* separately, and write down what comes to mind. As an image, sound, taste, or feeling comes to you, jot it down in the space provided below or in your magical journal.

PERSONAL LOVE CORRESPONDENCES

Colors:

Herbs:

Gemstones:

Sounds:

Animals:

Elements:

INSPIRATION, CREATIVITY, AND JOY PERSONAL CORRESPONDENCE EXERCISE

Complete the following imagery exercise to discover your own inspiration, creativity, and joy correspondences to use in future magical workings.

What you'll need

Journal

Writing utensil

Method

Go to your sacred space or sit in front of your altar. Make sure the area is cleansed and ground yourself. Take three deep breaths and close your eyes. Speak the word *joy* aloud over and over. As you do so, take notice of what images, animals, sounds, colors, tastes, and feelings come to you as you repeat the word *joy.* You could even say *animal for creativity, color for inspiration, herb for joy* separately, and write down what comes to mind. As an image, sound, taste, or feeling comes to you, jot it down in the space provided below or in your magical journal.

PERSONAL PROTECTION CORRESPONDENCES

Colors:

Herbs:

Gemstones:

Sounds:

Animals:

Elements:

Correspondence Intuition Exercise

What you'll need

Herbs (fresh or in packaging)

Journal

Writing utensil

Crystals

Candles in a variety of colors

Method

Take the intention exercises a step further and grab a variety of herbs. Sit on the floor and begin by spreading the herbs around you. Saying the word of an intention like *protection* three times aloud, close your eyes and hover your hands over the herbs. Slowly move your hands from left to right, keeping your eyes squeezed shut. When you sense a vibration or warm feeling in your fingertips or if your intuition tells you to stop moving your hands, open your eyes and record the item underneath. Repeat the exercise with the crystals, candles, and any other items you've chosen.

INTUITION CORRESPONDENCES

Herbs:

Crystals:

Candles:

Additional correspondence:

Additional correspondence:

Additional correspondence:

13

SPELL WORK

ONE OF THE FIRST THINGS that comes to mind when a person hears the word *witch* is *spell*. In fact, when I was young and wanted to be a witch, I thought one of the best ways to be one was if I did spells. I remember writing out rhymes and incantations and mixing together dirt and herbs and pretending to be a witch mixing ingredients in a cauldron. One of my first memories of kitchen magic was in my Nana and Peep's kitchen mixing together water, flour, and herbs to create *magic bread* to make me taller. It tasted terrible and unfortunately didn't work. I never grew past four foot eleven inches.

Some people are turned off when they hear the word *spell*, thinking it's some working of the Devil. We can thank pop culture and fearmongering religions for that misconception. In reality, nearly anyone can learn to cast a spell. You can consider yourself a witch and cast spells, you can follow any religious path and cast spells, or you can hold no religious beliefs at all and cast spells. There's no need to be initiated into a coven, no need to dedicate yourself to a certain pantheon of gods and goddess, or even wear the label of a witch in order to cast a spell. All you need is yourself, an intention and will, patience, and some tools (if you want) for an added boost of magic. Although we are used to seeing elaborate spells portrayed on television or on social media, spells don't need to be complicated or include difficult-to-acquire materials to be effective. The magic truly comes from you.

Before we get into the details of casting spells, I want to chat a bit about tools you may wish to acquire (not required at all!), sigil creation to enhance your spells, and candle magic—a common and relatively simple type of spell crafting. It just so happens to be one of my favorites.

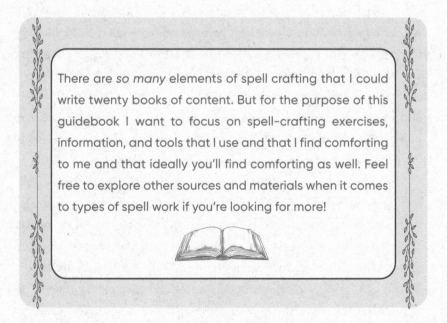

There are *so many* elements of spell crafting that I could write twenty books of content. But for the purpose of this guidebook I want to focus on spell-crafting exercises, information, and tools that I use and that I find comforting to me and that ideally you'll find comforting as well. Feel free to explore other sources and materials when it comes to types of spell work if you're looking for more!

Spell Crafting Tools

In witchcraft, tools are used to direct and manipulate energy, to communicate with guides and ancestors, and to get our intentions across. Although you can practice without tools, as all you really need is your intention and personal power, many witches like the tangible aspect of using tools.

Many people who cast spells feel that the best tools are the ones they either receive from others, grow in the garden, or personally make themselves. Others believe tools you purchase from New Age/witchy shops and herbs you pick up at the grocery store are just as effective. I'm here to tell you both ways of thinking are valid. Because tools are supplements to our own will and determination (the only true things we need to cast spells), you decide how many and what kind of tools to acquire. Personally, when I have too many tools, I get a bit over-whelmed, so make sure the ones you do choose to use have meaning to you. Here are some common tools used for spell work.

* **ATHAME:** This is a ritual dagger with a double-edged blade and a white or black handle. Many witches and magical practitioners engrave candles or cut physical and energetic cords with this tool. It's also used when casting a circle, stirring ingredients together, or invoking the elements or deities.

* **WAND:** The witch's wand is a tool traditionally carved from the wood of the hazel, rowan, willow, or ash tree and can be adorned with crystals and other stones. It's used to cast a circle, direct energy, stir ingredients together, or draw magical symbols in the dirt or sand. It is thought to be a sacred tool to all gods and goddesses.

✳ PENTACLE: The pentacle is a flat disc of silver, brass, wood, or clay portraying the five-pointed star known as a pentagram. It's used for balancing the elements as the elements and spirit are represented by the five points, for protection against negative entities and energies, and as a grounding tool to grasp onto after spells have been performed.

✳ CAULDRON: Long associated with witches, the cauldron is traditionally made of iron and also combines the power of all four elements. Its three legs symbolize the three main phases of the moon, the three stages of the divine feminine (maiden, mother, crone), and the triad of mind, body, and spirit. Cauldrons are used for a variety of purposes including fire rituals, brewing potions, burning incense, holding candles, and as altar décor.

✳ CHALICE: The chalice is a tool associated with the element of water, as it's a vessel for liquids. It's traditionally made of silver, glass, crystal, or wood and used as a cup for wine to leave as an offering. Many practitioners use the chalice to blend potions, mix herbs together, and drink from.

✳ ALTAR BELL: Traditionally used to indicate the beginning and concluding of a ritual, an altar bell is a small bell made of brass, silver, or glass. Many people ring an altar bell to dispel any negative energy, to reset tarot- or oracle-card decks with a sound cleansing, or to drive away mischievous entities.

✳ BESOM: This is a small broom used to cleanse (by sweeping out) an area. It's often used before and after a ritual, ceremony, or spell work, and it's often adorned with ribbon, crystals, and other charms. Many witches hang a besom next to their door, bristles up, or over their door for protection.

✳ GRIMOIRE: This is a magical journal of sorts where you keep notes about witchcraft that you can come back to again and again—personal correspondences, rituals, spells, herb and crystal information, and craft rules. Grimoires are frequently passed down through generations.

✳ BOOK OF SHADOWS: Like the grimoire, this is a magical journal of sorts, but where a grimoire is more of a reference book, a Book of Shadows recounts personal experiences with magic—reflections on spells, inner thoughts about your spiritual journey, specific card pulls and reflections of those, and more personal information in general.

✳ CRYSTALS AND STONES: Crystals and stones—some of the oldest tools on our planet—are used in rituals and spells for their energy and corresponding properties to your intention.

✳ MORTAR AND PESTLE: Used to crush herbs, plants, and other ingredients for use in spell work or even incense, mortars and pestles can be made of stone or wood.

Sigils

A sigil is a type of symbol used in magic to give a bit of extra oomph to a spell or ritual. These symbols have been around for thousands of years, going as far back as ancient times, where people would use drawings and symbols to communicate their desires and connect with the spirit realm. It's a drawing that represents a specific idea or intention that, once activated, can magnify the intention. Creating a sigil involves taking a present-tense statement of intention and condensing it down to a symbol which then represents that desire. That symbol is then charged and used in spell work and rituals to bring the desired outcome to fruition. Here's how to create a sigil:

1. Think about a desire you have. Make sure you are clear about this intention. Write the intention down in a present-tense phrase. For example, if you're seeking peace in your life you may write down *I am at peace with my life*. Like I always say, make sure you keep it simple and try not to include too many words and details.

2. Next you eliminate any vowels and repeating letters from your statement. Going with the example above, *I am at peace with my life*, you'd have the following letters left: M T P C W H L F.

3. Next, you'll arrange those letters to form some sort of symbol. Feel free to capitalize letters, lower case them, write them backward, use cursive—whatever calls to you. Here is the sigil I created using the letters from my initial peace statement.

4. Charge your sigil with energy by holding the sigil in your left hand and then covering it with your right. Close your eyes and focus on your intention, visualizing the desired outcome while grasping tightly onto your sigil.
5. Now it's time to put the sigil to use.

PRACTICE YOUR SIGIL CREATION

Statement of intent:

Letters left:

Your symbol:

WAYS TO USE YOUR SIGIL

There are many ways to use sigils in magic. You can incorporate them into your spells and rituals by etching them into a candle. You can stir the symbol with your spoon into your morning coffee or tea. You can simply meditate with the sigil in your hands. You can place the sigil on your altar as a reminder of your desired manifestation. You can also create jewelry out of your sigil as a reminder of your intention. Or you can write them in places hidden to others—on the bottom of your altar or under your front door mat or, like me, you can have it written on the back of your Book of Shadows or stitched onto your altar cloth to enhance magical workings.

Whether you are new to magic or an experienced practitioner, sigils offer a boost to your magic and put a personal touch on your practice. After all, no two sigils are the same.

Candle Magic

As we discussed in chapter 6 (the balance tenet), one of the simplest and most popular forms of spell work is candle magic. The candle is a focus for your mind. It's a point of concentration, so when you're working toward a specific goal or intention, the candle serves as a focus and allows you to concentrate on that intention wholeheartedly. The first step in crafting a candle spell is setting an intention. And really the first step in any type of spell work is setting an intention.

CHOOSING A COLOR

Candle magic and color magic go hand in hand. Oftentimes the candle you choose to work with is chosen for its color correspondence to your intention. And color magic goes beyond candles and can be incorporated into all areas of your life. Think about your home—you chose to paint and decorate with specific colors because they elicit some sort of response within. And what about your clothing? There are some days I'm drawn to wearing something bright and colorful, while other days I'm called to stay neutral. Creating a candle spell with a colorful candle is just as simple and as intuitive as decorating your house or dressing yourself in the morning. Choose a color based on your intention and then let the magic begin! Here are some common candle colors and magical intentions they support. (Note: The best candles for short-term spells would be chime candles, and long-term spells where you'll burn the candle many times over require a taper or jar candle.)

✳ PINK: love, friendship

✳ RED: courage, lust, love, passion

✳ ORANGE: attraction, creativity, inspiration, vitality

✳ DARK BLUE: protection, vulnerability

✳ LIGHT BLUE: health, patience, communication

✳ BROWN: earth, family, hearth and home

✳ BLACK: protection, banishment

✳ PURPLE: magic, ambition, power

✳ LAVENDER: connection to spirit, peace, inner calm

✳ GOLD: sun, abundance, joy

✳ SILVER: moon, intuition

✳ GREEN: abundance, prosperity, money workings

✳ YELLOW: confidence, joy, happiness

✳ WHITE: purity (can be a substitute for *all* colors)

DRESSING A CANDLE

Once you've set an intention and chosen a color, the next step is to dress the candle in corresponding oils and herbs. This is also a time you can inscribe the candle with a symbol or sigil of your choosing. To dress a candle, do the following:

1. Select an essential oil(s) that corresponds with your chosen intention or an oil you intuitively choose for this working. If you've chosen an oil that shouldn't be handled on its own, make sure you dilute it with a carrier oil, such as jojoba, grapeseed, or almond oil.
2. Choose one or two dried herbs that correspond with your chosen intention or herbs you intuitively choose for this working.
3. Holding the candle in your left hand, gently rub your essential oil blend in upward strokes on the candle. Be sure to leave a quarter inch of unoiled candle near the wick, as the oil could easily catch flame. While you're rubbing the oil on the candle, repeat in your head or aloud your intended outcome.
4. Next, sprinkle your herb blend on the oiled part of the candle, then again rub in upward strokes. You may also roll the candle in the herbs, but be sure to rub them into the candle until they're stuck in place. Again, say in your head or aloud the intended outcome of the spell.
5. You're ready to put the candle to work.

MAKING YOUR CANDLE MAGIC

Now that your candle has been chosen and dressed, it's time to get to the magic-making. There are many ways you can go about using the candle. You can simply burn the candle with the chosen intention in mind. You can write down anything you'd like to see leave your life and burn the paper in the flame, releasing what no longer serves you. You can enchant jewelry or other crystals by holding the object above the flame while speaking your desire for the piece and the desired outcome when you wear or carry it. The dressing of the candle can be the spell in and of itself, and there's no need at all to light the wick; simply place the candle on your altar or somewhere in your sacred space as a reminder of the intention you set. You can also light color-coordinating candles and chant an incantation that explains your intentions. For example, you may light red and pink candles (representing love) and say:

> *Candles, I light this night, bring me love within my sight.*
> *Goddess of love I ask of you, send me someone kind and*
> *true. Help me find my one true love, so below*
> *and as above.*

Whatever you do though, make sure you work with fire safely. Don't forget to have a fire extinguisher handy and always work with a fire-safe dish. And naturally, never leave a flame unattended.

Truly, you can make the candle magic in whatever way you see fit.

Candle Magic Template

Intention:

Candle color:

Sigil or sign:

Oils and herbs:

Crystals and other tools:

Spell:

THE FLAME TELLS A STORY

When you're working with candle magic, the size and movement of your candle's flame has a story of its own. A tall, steady flame during a working indicates the spell is going well and that your intentions are clear and concise. A short, dancing flame could mean the work isn't going so well or your intention is unclear. Make sure you adjust accordingly.

Book of Shadows/Grimoire

I know I already talked about the difference between a Book of Shadows and a grimoire, but something I've been noticing over time is that the two terms are used interchangeably. No matter how you want to label it, make sure you have some sort of magical journal to record you spells and your successes and failures with them. Although we all want to think our magical workings work every time, that's not the case. Refer back to the section on magical journaling from part 1 for types of magical journals. This may be the perfect time to start one dedicated to your spell work!

Now let's get into creating your own spells.

Spell Creation

This next section is all about creating your own individual and unique spells, utilizing a variety of elements we've discussed throughout this book to make these spells as powerful as they can be. For each spell you write, you'll want to reference all the exercises you've completed throughout this comfy cozy witchcraft guidebook, paying particular attention to the intentions you've set for your magical practice, your nonnegotiables, and the personal correspondences you've created.

What is a spell? A spell is a way you can bring your desires to reality. They often take the form of spoken words mixed with ingredients to enhance the working and potential prayers or help from your spirit team. I want to start by saying there truly is no right or wrong way to create a spell. I think that so many people get caught up in the *Am I doing it right?* mentality that they never try. I also think that there are many practitioners who are too afraid to create their own spells so they simply rely on the tried and true spells and rituals created by others. Although there is definitely merit in performing the spells of others, there is much more power behind creating the spells yourself. Keep in mind, spells do not need to be long, elaborate, and adorned with rhyming quatrains and incantations. What matters is what the words and correspondences and symbols you're using mean to *you*. It's much more effective to have a short and sweet spell that means something to you rather than recite and re-create words written by someone else, someone who has no idea of your desired outcomes and intentions. Let's look at the "ingredients" you'll want to consider when creating a spell.

✳ INTENTION: I must say that of all the items you'll see listed here, the intention is the one nonnegotiable. You need to set an intention to your magical workings or else they have no direction.

✳ MOON PHASE: Refer to the opening chapters when I discussed which moon phases are compatible with which types of workings. Keep in mind that that is a reference point and not something you need to follow. If you're feeling a releasing spell during the waxing moon, then go for it!

✳ TOOLS: You decide if and what tools you want to use during your spell. If you're doing an energetic cord cutting, you may want to consider an athame or pair of scissors, but your pointer and middle finger in a scissor shape will do the trick if need be. Tools are utilized to enhance and supplement your spell work, but they're not necessities.

✳ MATERIALS: Think about your intention and then select corresponding candles, herbs, oils, crystals, and so on, if you so choose. Every ingredient you select should have a purpose, so don't grab a labradorite tumble because you read somewhere you needed it. Choose materials that are meaningful to *you* and to *your intention*.

ANATOMY OF A SPELL

Now that we have our intention and chosen tools and materials, the next step is to look at a spell breakdown. Every magical practitioner has their own method of performing spells. I'm going to share with you what has worked for me. As usual, feel free to adapt this template however you see fit. Most spells are constructed with the same elements in mind.

1. SETTING THE SCENE. This is the first step. You already have your tools and have identified your purpose or intention. Now it's time to set up your space for spell work. Ideally you're performing this in a space that is sacred to you—the sacred space you created for yourself in front of an altar or out in nature. Set up the tools and materials you've gathered in a way that feels natural and intuitive to you.

2. GROUNDING AND PROTECTING YOURSELF. Your sacred space is prepared for spell work, so it's time to get to what I consider the basis for any magical working—grounding. You can do this by closing your eyes and envisioning roots growing up from the ground and running through your body, rooting you in place. You can do this by performing some deep breathing exercises. Or you can do a short meditation grounding and centering you in this space. This is also the time to call in protection. You can visualize a bubble of protective light surrounding you and your sacred space or you can cast a circle of protection. (See page 114.)

3. CALLING IN HELP. Although this part is not a requirement of any spell, calling in help from your guides, angels, elements, deities, ancestors, and the like is something that many people choose to do. Simply ask these helpers to assist you in your spell work for your highest good. At the conclusion of your working, make sure you thank and then release the guides.

4. **PERFORMING THE SPELL.** Now that the scene is set—you've grounded yourself and called in any help—it's time for the magic to begin. Perhaps you've set up a ritual of candle magic. Maybe you're creating a spell jar with a variety of ingredients based on an intention. Whatever it is, you want to make sure you have prepared words for the spell. The magic is in the words you speak and the intention behind those words, so be specific with them. Keep in mind it's not necessary to rhyme.

5. **CLOSING THE SPELL.** Close the spell by thanking and releasing your guides (if you brought them in). Close the spell by saying something like, "The spell is now complete. So be it."

6. **PUTTING INTENTION TO ACTION.** So many practitioners think they're finished once the spell has been cast, but in reality, the spell has just begun. Magic is the combination of spell work and action. If you've completed a spell for financial abundance and prosperity, you need to now put in the work. If you've completed a spell for self-love and compassion, you need to now honor that work by partaking in self-love practices like affirmations, journaling, or ritual baths. The work doesn't end when the spell does.

CASTING A CIRCLE

Before you begin a spell, it's a good idea to cast a circle around yourself and your sacred space to contain the magic and to protect you from distractions and any outside influences. You can use something physical to show the circular boundary like a rope, string, candles, or a circle of salt. You could also simply walk around the circumference to do this or you can "draw" the circle with a wand, athame, or your hand or finger. While casting the circle, work deosil (clockwise) and say, "I cast this circle to contain my magic and protect me from all." When you're finished with your spell, release the circle by working widdershins (counterclockwise) and say, "The spell has been cast and the circle is released."

Spell Template

This template is a starting point to document your magical workings. You can tweak it as you see fit, but it's a good idea to record any details about your spell in your magical journal so you can reference them in the future, reflect on their outcome, and adapt them for future workings.

Date:

Day of the week:

Moon phase:

Place:

Ritual/spell name:

Purpose/intention:

Ingredients and tools:

Grounding and protection:

Guides and helpers:

Method:

Incantations, prayers, or rhymes:

During this ritual, I felt:

After this ritual, I felt:

Further actions:

Reflections:

My Spells

COMFY COZY MAGIC

COMFY COZY MAGIC IS, AFTER all, my favorite kind of magic and well . . . my witchy namesake. And although all of what you've seen throughout this book is cozy in nature, I felt a chapter dedicated to my favorite cozy magical things would be appreciated by all you like-minded reader friends. In this chapter I'll also share with you a few rituals, spells, and information about divination forms and animals you may like to incorporate into your own unique practice. Let's start with what I believe to be the coziest and most magical season of all—fall.

Autumn Magic

For me, the most magical time of the year coincides with the coziest time of the year—autumn. I'm fortunate to have true fall weather where I live in Pennsylvania. I know not all witches are as lucky as I am to experience the cool, crisp mornings and chilly evenings wrapped up in a blanket while sitting around a bonfire. But there is something innately magical with the autumn season—the vibrant burnt orange, yellow, and burgundy hues of leaves highlighted by the moon's glow, that feeling of both mystery and calm in the air, and the smell of dying leaves while everyone gears up for the Samhain/Halloween festival. The heat of summer has died down, so now I can truly embrace long walks through local forests and parks, enjoy watching the squirrels and foxes in my neighborhood and local lands, and spend time turning over my garden.

Although I'm writing this particular chapter toward the end of August, I have to tell you the past few mornings have felt like fall mornings. I've woken up to temperatures in the low sixties, and although not as chilly as a fall morning, it certainly gets me in the mood for fall. Honestly, once Lughnasadh hits I'm in the fall mood. In fact, next week, I'll be switching out the window décor in my shop from summer to a fall aesthetic. I can't wait! I especially love the transition to fall as we've gone from my least favorite season to my most favorite.

Cozy Fall Rituals

Here's a list of some of my favorite cozy autumn rituals.

* Create an outdoor altar of pumpkins, leaves, acorns, and nuts.

* Pick some flowers to set inside your home.

* Search for local fauna.

* Pack and enjoy a picnic in nature.

* Go apple picking.

* Take your magical journaling outside.

* Decorate your porch with lanterns, gourds, leaves, and
  mushrooms.

* Bake fruit pies to honor the season.

* Spend time journaling for gratitude.

* Make a simmer pot of apples, cloves, cinnamon, and nutmeg.

* Make a cornhusk dolly.

Tea and Coffee Magic

A staple to this comfy cozy witch's magical routine is tea and coffee
magic. I've mentioned before that each morning I intentionally stir
cinnamon and honey in my coffee for warmth and protection and
to welcome sweetness and kindness to my day. Much of the magic
of sipping on tea and coffee comes from the mindful actions of preparing the leaves/grounds and water, inhaling the aromas, and tasting the herbs. There is something meditative to sipping on a warm
beverage. I also enjoy mindful moments in the late afternoon and
evenings sipping on tea while curled up on my sofa with a good book
and fluffy blanket. I find myself especially excited to enjoy my cups
of tea during fall when I am more called to do tea-leaf readings as
part of my morning ritual.

Tea-Leaf Reading Ritual

Here's a fun tea-leaf reading ritual so you can have a bit of cozy, magical fun yourself.

WHAT YOU'LL NEED

1 teaspoon of loose-leaf tea (I personally like oolong)
Teacup (or a mug) and saucer
Boiling water

METHOD

1. Place the tea in the teacup (do not add milk or sweetener).
2. Pour the boiling water into the teacup on top of the tea.
3. Allow the tea to steep 3 to 4 minutes.
4. Slowly sip on the liquid with a question or "guidance for the day" in mind.
5. Sip on the tea until the leaves begin sticking to your lips. Make sure there's a splash of liquid left. Flip over your cup on the saucer and spin it three times to the right.
6. Flip the teacup back over with the handle toward you and read the contents.

Reading the Leaves

Symbols are seen and interpreted in the cup and you can either interpret what you're seeing using your own eyes and intuition or you can use the following common symbols as a guide.

ANIMALS: The meaning of animals generally goes off of culturally accepted representations of those animals. Birds will represent freedom, travel, and news coming to you. Fish are considered lucky, but one that appears dead is unlucky. An elephant represents good health and longevity, while a bee indicates that you will be busy with hard work. Butterflies are symbols of fate, cats are a message to beware of secrets coming to light, while a dog is, of course, indicative of a good friend and companion. An angel means that you are protected and watched over.

LETTERS: Generally letters are taken to represent someone with that initial. Look for figures around the letter or even faces to try and decipher who it can be. Together with the other images, you can then try and piece together who may be reaching out and what their message might be.

OBJECTS: Many symbols are self-explanatory, such as a cross indicating a blockage of some kind, a heart representing new love or harmonious relationship, or a lightbulb or candle indicating new ideas and insights coming to you. A bed can represent a need to rest while triangles and clovers are considered omens of good fortune. The sun is always a symbol of success and happiness entering your life, and apples represent knowledge. If you see a kite or horseshoe—make a wish! A dagger, knife, or sword can represent danger or backstabbing. Often the tea leaves will arrange themselves simply in lines or dots. Lines can indicate a journey or being chained, depending on the thickness and feeling you gauge from them, while dots can foretell an upcoming increase or flurry of activity.

NUMBERS: Often numbers are said to indicate time, so when the surrounding messages will come to fruition. This can be days, weeks, or months, depending on where in the cup they are.

Animal Magic

If you listen to my podcast, then you certainly know about my three best girls—Gia, Ries, and River. These dogs are my fur babies, and although I don't consider any of them familiars, they are very, very connected to me and my practice. I mean Ries is with me in my sacred space pretty much any time I'm in there, and I know you all have heard her in the background of the podcast barking at passing delivery vehicles and letting me know when she wants to go for a walk.

Witches see cats and other animals as allies, creatures to help comfort us in times of need, and many magical people have a strong connection with animals of all kinds, like they do with nature. My three furry friends are here for companionship, comfort, and a good laugh once in a while (thank you, Ries!) though others (like me, again) have animals who have made themselves known as spirit guides—animals who appear during meditation and divination to give advice, guidance, and inspiration and for strength.

And there are many practitioners whose animals take the role of familiars—an animal that is spiritually connected to its owner and takes part in magical workings. Many familiars are guardians and protectors, sent to assist their *person* with magic. It's also been thought that since familiars are psychically connected to their person they can communicate their thoughts and feelings to one another.

Although my girls do curl up next to me while I'm doing magical workings, I find their magic comes mostly in the form of being a comfort when I'm feeling down or anxious. Know that animals do not need to be considered familiars to supply comfort and a touch of magic to a person's life.

When it comes to encountering animals in general, it's important to realize that animal allies are all around us—in our homes, in nature, in our dreams—and they kindly bestow their magical gifts on us whether we realize it or not. Although I've done a brief overview of what various animals represent in the magical glossary at the end of the book, below you will find more detailed information about animals we commonly encounter. If you are searching in parts of your life for qualities these animals possess, place a representation of that animal on your altar or sacred space.

BEE: Bees represent collaboration, perseverance, and sweetness (hello, honey!), and when a bee appears it's a sign of a potential new opportunity. You can honor bees by not harming them, by adding honey to your teas and baked goods, and by planting a pollinator garden full of their favorite flowers.

BIRD: Although various birds represent specific qualities, birds in general correspond with freedom, joy, messages from the ancestors and spirit team, dreams, and anything to do with thoughts or ideas. Honor bird allies with clean birdbaths, birdhouses to protect them from the elements, and bird feeders hung in your outdoor space and filled frequently.

BUTTERFLY/DRAGONFLY: Representative of transformation, rebirth, magic, and imagination, butterflies and dragonflies are known to bring messages from your spirit team. If you see these beautiful winged creatures over and over again, your guides may be trying to communicate something with you, so listen. You can honor them by planting butterfly bushes, spending time near a pond or lake and watching their beauty, or hanging their images in your sacred space.

CAT: A mystical and favorite animal to witches, cats represent magical power, intuition, wisdom, mystery, and longevity. They also represent freedom, independence, moon energy, and cleanliness and are connected to the spirit world. You can honor cats by putting out warm milk, by giving strays a loving place to stay out of the elements, and through working with the Greek goddess Hecate.

DEER: One of my closest animal allies, deer symbolize beauty, gentleness, awareness of surroundings, a connection to the earth element, grounding, and mindfulness. They're also known to represent grace, kindness, and love. If you spot a deer, it means your spirit team is watching out for you. You can honor deer by being attentive while you drive and by leaving them at peace in their natural habitat.

DOG: It's no surprise to learn dogs represent loyalty, friendship, compassion, unconditional love, playfulness, and protection. My dogs do all these things for me, and I honor them by showing love and respect and giving lots of cuddles, belly rubs, and daily walks. You can honor the properties of a dog through kind gestures toward others and by not taking yourself too seriously.

FISH: Like birds—although there are properties for each kind of fish—fish, in general, represent abundance, awareness of your higher self, and connection to your emotions and deep feelings. Because they're from the sea, fish associate strongly with the water element and can help when working with emotions. Honor fish by feeding them and by tapping into your emotions.

FOX: My favorite animal, as many of you know, the fox is often an animal-spirit guide and represents cleverness, hidden thoughts and emotions, cunning, and intelligence and is known to have a strong connection to the spirit world. Also symbolic of spirituality, creation, and the afterlife, foxes help people navigate their own spiritual path. Honor foxes by leaving them in their natural habitat and by connecting to your spiritual side.

HUMMINGBIRD: A very common animal guide, hummingbirds represent sweetness, happiness, joy, ancestor connection, and high vibrations. You can honor them by hanging a feeder specifically for them outside your home, just be sure to keep the nectar fresh by thoroughly cleaning the feeder each week.

OWL: Another animal sacred to the witch, the owl represents lunar energy, the divine feminine, wisdom, intuition, and the afterlife. You can honor owls by continuing your learning on your spiritual path and by hanging owl imagery in your sacred space or near your altar to invite in wisdom and occult knowledge.

Meditation to Call in an Animal Guide

Adapted from my book *Hearth and Home Witchcraft*, this easy meditation to call in an animal guide is one I knew I just had to share. Animal-spirit guides bring great peace and comfort to the lives of witches, pagans, and nonmagical peoples and have done so for centuries. If you haven't yet met an animal on your spirit team or have been wishing to do so, complete the following meditation to call them in.

WHAT YOU'LL NEED

1 white candle
Candle-safe dish or holder
Lighter or matches
Journal or notebook
Writing utensil

METHOD

1. Find a comfortable place in your sacred space or outside in nature where you are alone and relaxed. Place your candle on a candle-safe dish and light it. Set it in front of you.
2. Close your eyes and take three deep breaths. After the third exhale, say:

   Animal guide, show yourself to me during this meditation.
   Help me as I walk my path, bringing me strength, comfort,
   support, and guidance all for my highest good.

3. Envision yourself walking along a path in the forest. Notice the plants and trees surrounding you as you walk deeper and deeper into the canopied trees. Notice the scents, the sounds. Suddenly, you hear a rustling up ahead and a clearing appears. What is making that sound? What animal do you see? Take a step toward it and reach out your hand. Ask what message it has for you.

4. After you've received the message, thank your animal. Turn around and walk back on the path by which you came.

5. Slowly open your eyes. Take a few moments to write in your magical journal about your experience. What animal did you see, if any? Did they have a message for you? What was the message? How did it make you feel to be in their presence? What colors, images, or scents were in your meditation?

Note: If you didn't connect with an animal during this meditation, try it again and again until you do. I'd been doing meditations to connect with one of my guides for more than a year before I ever saw him. Like anything good and magical, it takes time, practice, and patience.

Book and Word Magic

As an author and avid reader of books of all kinds, it's no surprise that a form of cozy magic in my life is book magic. Books have the ability to wash our cares away, to transport us to other worlds, and to allow us to be fully engrossed in something tangible and in the present moment. Nothing says *comfy cozy* more than snuggling up in my favorite chair with a good book in my hands, dogs in my lap, and tea on the coffee table. And the power words wield is nothing short of magic. Think of the words you weave through the charms and incantations you use in spell work.

And when I think of book magic, I'm not just thinking about books on witchcraft and magic. I'm also not talking about fiction books that are witchy-themed. Books and words in general hold so much power. How can you be more present and mindful than when

WHAT ARE CHARMS AND INCANTATIONS?

We already know that spells are a way of drawing on the strength of the unseen and using your magical actions and words to bring an intention to reality. But where do written words come in? Incantations are used in many spells to give the spell verbal power. They are often beautiful and rhythmic chants, prayers, or strings of words that are spoken with passion and repeated for emphasis. Spoken charms are any magical words, phrases, chants, or even incantations spoken with the intention of protection. Although tangible charms are objects that have been charged with magical energy to perform some sort of purpose, they are technically the words and phrases spoken in a spell.

you're engrossed in a good book? Reading is a naturally grounding experience, so it's also a great way to ground after performing a magical working.

Card Magic

A staple of my comfy cozy practice is divination. I practice some form of divination nearly every morning and longer divination rituals during the eight seasonal sabbats. Although I've played around with most forms of divination over the years, I always come back to the tried-and-true card reading. My preference of oracle cards versus tarot has changed many, many times over the years (in fact, I'm on a bit of an oracle kick right now), but I wanted to distinguish the two as it's something I'm asked about often.

Originally used for games, much like playing cards today, tarot cards are a set of seventy-eight cards broken up into the major arcana (twenty-two cards that follow the fool's journey, representing stages of our life/archetypes) and the minor arcana (the suit cards—cups, swords, wands, and pentacles—fifty-six cards that represent everyday experiences, day-to-day events, people interacting with you in the present or near future). Every tarot deck has the same seventy-eight-card structure and basic imagery; however, different artists have put their own spins on the artwork and packaging of cards. But the foundation of every tarot deck is the same.

On the other hand, oracle cards can have any number of cards, on any number of themes and topics, and in general are a little more intuitive than tarot and more affirmative in nature. Most oracle-card decks come with a guidebook to help you better understand the imagery and meaning of the cards, which many new to card divination appreciate.

You don't need any special training in either of these forms of divination; however, a little background knowledge and research on the basic elements of the tarot would be helpful if that's where you want to start.

The Major Arcana

✳ 0—THE FOOL. Keywords: innocence, idealism, naiveté, and potential. The fool can be both positive and negative in that it represents a fresh childlike outlook but is also inexperienced and naïve.

✳ I—THE MAGICIAN. Keywords: achievement, power, and four elements. This is a true magician and represents skills and someone who possesses all the tools needed to achieve.

✳ II—THE HIGH PRIESTESS. Keywords: mystical, dreaming, and feminine side. She represents wisdom and intuition, and asks you to see what it is you cannot acknowledge.

✳ III—THE EMPRESS. Keywords: motherly, fertility, and creation. This loving mother figure is asking you to nurture others and to seek nurturing from the earth and loved ones.

✳ IV—THE EMPEROR. Keywords: authority, discipline, and rules. He represents a foil to the empress in his straightforward message to find structure in your life.

✳ V—THE HIEROPHANT. Keywords: Learning, religion, and conformity. This card represents a spiritual belief system and serves as a beacon of guidance and wisdom.

✳ VI—THE LOVERS. Keywords: harmony, love, and two sides. This card can represent a romantic relationship or a reconciliation within parts of yourself.

✴ VII—THE CHARIOT. Keywords: momentum, willpower, and balance. The chariot reminds us to keep everything in balance as we move forward in life. Find the balance of life.

✴ VIII—STRENGTH. Keywords: confidence, resilience, and protection. Strength is here to let us know we can get through a difficult situation if we're working hard to do so.

✴ IX—THE HERMIT. Keywords: solitude, peace, and going inward. This card asks you to go inward and reflect on a situation in order to gain clarity. Sometimes you just need to be alone and appreciate being there.

✴ X—WHEEL OF FORTUNE. Keywords: cyclical, happiness, and luck. The wheel reminds you that there are always ups on the other side of downs and that you can be guided through all parts of life with a joyful outcome.

✴ XI—JUSTICE. Keywords: truth, balance, and fairness. No matter the outcome, you will get what's coming to you. Be grateful.

✴ XII—THE HANGED MAN. Keywords: surrender and faith. Rather than struggle against things happening in your life, accept them. All is going as it needs to.

✴ XIII—DEATH. Keywords: transformation and change. Even if you're nervous about what's to come—good or bad—move on and put the past in the past.

✴ XIV—TEMPERANCE. Keywords: calm, self-control, and balance. Temperance reminds you to be patient and don't rush any decisions. Things will make sense in time.

* XV—THE DEVIL. Keywords: ignorance, ego, and danger. You're often your own worst enemy, so this card wants you to make sure you're not getting in your own way.

* XVI—TOWER. Keywords: rebirth, upheaval, and liberation. This is your wake-up call to make a change after an upheaval. There will be peace in the end.

* XVII—THE STAR. Keywords: hope, inspiration, and balance. You have your new beginning. There is much power in looking on the bright side.

* XVIII—THE MOON. Keywords: illusion, imagination, and unfamiliar. Things aren't entirely clear, so take some time to reflect. The moon asks you to look to your intuition.

* XIX—THE SUN. Keywords: glory, confidence, and illumination. The sun is here to say things are looking up and to remind you to be joyful. Abundance and success are here!

* XX—JUDGMENT. Keywords: possibilities and reflection. This is a reminder that the past is in the past, but sometimes it's important to reflect on what can be done differently.

* XXI—THE WORLD. Keywords: wholeness, fulfillment, and closure. The world reminds you that the goal has been reached. It's time to celebrate your success and acknowledge that all your hard work has paid off.

We'll quickly look at the various suits in the minor arcana and then keywords for each card for quick reference if you're just starting out with tarot or need a refresh. Again, I want to reiterate the importance of using your own intuition and discernment when doing any type of divination. Use this as a guide.

✳ SUIT OF CUPS: Cups is the suit of relationships—romantic, friendship, and relationship with yourself. Deeply connected to the water element and our emotions the suit of cups is ruled by emotions and matters of the heart and decisions made from the heart. While positive aspects of the cups suit include being in touch with your emotions, creativity, and thinking with the heart, there are negative aspects as well. These include being disengaged, being overly emotional, repressing emotions, setting unrealistic expectations, and romanticizing life to a point of living in a fantasy.

☆ ACE: potential in love, new relationships, and beginnings

☆ TWO: attraction, unity, and intimacy

☆ THREE: celebration and friendship

☆ FOUR: reflection, self-absorption, and ego

☆ FIVE: failure, grief, and regret

☆ SIX: memories and innocence

☆ SEVEN: choices and temptation

☆ EIGHT: disappointment and dissatisfaction

☆ NINE: fulfillment, joy, and satisfaction

☆ TEN: harmony and good relationships

☆ PAGE: potential and budding relationship

☆ KNIGHT: romance and fantasy

☆ QUEEN: nurture, motherly, and intuition

☆ KING: emotional balance and mature

✳ SUIT OF PENTACLES: Pentacles, sometimes referred to as the suite of coins or discs, deals with matters of the house and home—finances, work, prosperity, and family. Traditionally the suit of work for financial gain, pentacles speaks to practical and tangible matters and our basic needs and goals. Positive aspects of pentacles include success in business, trade, property, and money, and also include manifestation coming to fruition and prosperity. The negative aspects of the pentacles suit include possessiveness, materialism, envy, greed, and sacrificing other obligations like family and personal time to work.

☆ ACE: new work opportunity, potential, and prosperity

☆ TWO: adaptability, ability to juggle, and harmony

☆ THREE: collaboration and moving forward

☆ FOUR: success and material gain

☆ FIVE: poverty, loneliness, and loss

- ☆ **SIX:** charity, generosity, and receiving wealth
- ☆ **SEVEN:** fortune, investment, and anxiety over future
- ☆ **EIGHT:** skill honing and hard work
- ☆ **NINE:** inheritance, success, and accomplishment
- ☆ **TEN:** long-term success, wealth, and love of home
- ☆ **PAGE:** learning a new skill, good management, and motivation
- ☆ **KNIGHT:** hard work and trustworthy
- ☆ **QUEEN:** nurturing, generosity, and practical
- ☆ **KING:** confidence, leadership, and success

☆ **SUIT OF WANDS:** The suit of wands, associated with the element fire, is all about motivation, action, and creation. This is the suit that urges you to take action, serves as your inspiration, and pushes you to take that leap of faith to try a new endeavor—starting a business, trying a new hobby, making that big purchase, or stepping into that life change with confidence. The positive aspects of the wands suit include energy, motivation, and passion, especially when it comes to your personality. Its negative aspects are egotistical behavior, a lack of direction, creative blocks, and feeling like you don't have meaning.

- ☆ **ACE:** inspiration, creativity, and new opportunities
- ☆ **TWO:** decisions and planning

☆ THREE: collaboration, exploration, and progress

☆ FOUR: accomplishment, early success, and peace

☆ FIVE: roadblocks and competition

☆ SIX: victory, pride, support, and confidence

☆ SEVEN: perseverance, delay, and victory

☆ EIGHT: swiftness, action, and quick pace

☆ NINE: courage and determination

☆ TEN: responsibility, completion, and potential struggle

☆ PAGE: curiosity and discovery

☆ KNIGHT: passionate, energetic, and hasty

☆ QUEEN: success, power, and determination

☆ KING: visionary and leadership

✳ SUIT OF SWORDS: As its material suggests, swords indicate conflicts, but not physical conflicts, rather conflicts within the mind. Often associated with wit and intelligence, the sword suit, associated with the element of air, shows the power of intellect and the delicate balance between that and power and how those two elements can be, indeed, double-edged—you guessed it— swords. Positive aspects include action, change, force, power, ambition, courage, and conflict. Its negative aspects include anger, guilt, resentment, lack of compassion, and verbal and mental abuse.

✩ ACE: breakthroughs, new ideas, and success

✩ TWO: difficult decisions and avoidance

✩ THREE: despair, pain, heartbreak, and grief

✩ FOUR: rest, relaxation, and recuperation

✩ FIVE: conflict, disagreements, and defeat

✩ SIX: transition, releasing baggage, and change

✩ SEVEN: deception, manipulation, and strategy

✩ EIGHT: negative thoughts, self-doubt, and restriction

✩ NINE: anxiety, fear, and depression

✩ TEN: betrayal, tragedy, and crisis

✩ PAGE: new ideas, curiosity, and thirst for knowledge

✩ KNIGHT: ambitious, fast-thinking, and wit

✩ QUEEN: direct communication, clear boundaries, and hard truths

✩ KING: power, intellectual authority, and mental clarity

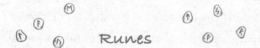

Runes

Another form of divination I do often is working with runes, specifically the Elder Futhark. Not only do I cast runes as a form of guidance, but I also use the runic symbols in my magical workings as symbols similar to how I use sigils.

Originally a system of writing for a variety of Germanic languages even before the Latin alphabet became dominant, runes were used not only for communication but for divination, protection, and other forms of magic. The word *rune* translates to *secret* or *whisper*, and it was thought only the wisest of men and women were able to interpret them. In Norse mythology, the god Odin was responsible for bringing knowledge of the runes to the gods and then to humanity. In all honesty, there are varying thoughts and opinions on the usage of runes throughout history, but one thing is for certain—many witches choose to use them in their practices for divination and magical workings. You can get to know the runes and their meanings from doing daily readings similar to a daily oracle- or tarot-card pull. You can also cast the runes by shaking them in a bag and then pouring them out on a plan white or black cloth. Which runes face you and ask you to work with them? When I work with runes, I like to hold the bag of runes in my left hand and shake them gently while asking a guided question like: What do I need to see today? How should I approach *a specific situation*? What type of energy will I encounter today? I pull as many runes from the bag as I see fit and then journal about them and their relation to what is going on in my life.

I also work with runes during candle magic by etching runic symbols in candles for an added intentional boost, or I draw them on objects. I have a small wooden platform on my writing space at home where I've drawn the berkano rune symbol, which to me represents the birth of creative ideas. You can also draw runic symbols on pieces of paper to tuck into charm bags, poppets, or other magical crafts.

Here's a basic overview of the Elder Futhark runes (the first written alphabet of people who'd come to be known as the Vikings) and their meanings. Obviously if you get any other intuitive hits from specific runes, then work with that.

✳ FEHU means *livestock* and represents wealth, abundance, success, security, and fertility.

✳ URUZ means *bull* and represents strength, tenacity, courage, and freedom.

✳ THURISAZ means *thorn* and represents reaction, defense, conflict, and regeneration.

✳ ANSUZ means *breath* and represents communication, understanding, and inspiration.

✳ RAIDHO means *journey* and represents travel, rhythm, decisions, and spontaneity.

✳ KENNAZ means *torch* and represents vision, creativity, inspiration, and vitality.

✳ GEBO means *gift* and represents balance, exchange, partnership, and relationships.

✳ WUNJO means *joy* and represents pleasure, comfort, success, and prosperity.

✳ HAGALAZ means *hail* and represents nature, wrath, obstacles, and being tested.

✳ NAUTHIZ means *need* and represents restriction, conflict, willpower, and endurance.

* ISA means *ice* and represents clarity, challenges, introspection, and patience.

* JERA means *year* and represents cycles, completion, changes, and harvest.

* EIHWAZ means *yew* and represents balance, enlightenment, and death.

* PERTHRO means *dice* and represents fate, chance, mystery, and secrets.

* ALGIZ means *elk* and represents protection, instinct, defense, and guardianship.

* SOWILO means *sun* and represents health, victory, cleansing, and wholeness.

* TIWAZ means *creator* and represents masculinity, justice, leadership, and logic.

* BERKANO means *birch tree* and represents fertility, rebirth, healing, and femininity.

* EHWAZ means *horse* and represents transportation, movement, progress, and change.

* MANNAZ means *humanity* and represents friendship, society, cooperation, and intelligence.

* LAGUZ means *water* and represents intuition, emotions, flow, dreams, and renewal.

* INGUZ means *seed* and represents growth, goals, change, and hearth and home.

✳ OTHALA means *household* and represents ancestry, possessions, experience, and value.

✳ DAGAZ means *dawn* and represents awakening, hope, certainty, and illumination.

Crafting Magic

It will be no surprise to many of you that I find comfort and magic in crafting. Over the years I've done much crafting in my practice: created room-cleansing sprays, ritual bath salts, herbal rubs and tinctures, magical journaled (of course), practiced knot magic with witches' bells and ladders, *attempted* to sew my own tarot pouches (I'll let the professional seamstresses do that! Haha), created pagan prayer beads for a variety of sabbats, intentions, and deities, and so much more. I've also crafted items over the years to honor the seasonal celebrations: wreaths at Ostara, a mini maypole at Beltane, a Brigid's cross at Imbolc, garlands at Mabon, rune ornaments for the Yule tree, altar cloths at Samhain, and more. There is so much power in getting your hands on materials and knotting and folding and stirring in intentions. And when you really think about it, a lot of what we do at our altars or in our sacred spaces could be considered crafting magic—altar décor, spell jar and wand creation, charm-bag and packet spell work, incense blends, sigil construction, magical bath products . . . you get the idea.

You can do a simple Google search for witchy crafts or even ask some of your trusted friends you hopefully met when I challenged you to join a magical group back in part 1 of the book. Now let's have a little cozy magical fun with making a cloth poppet.

Magical Crafting a Poppet

Poppet magic involves using an object that represents someone or something for which you're working the spell. Poppets, or dolls, are a great type of representation or sympathetic magic. They're small figurines constructed from paper, wood, cloth, or clay that are shaped into human form. (Roughly shaped is okay!) Keep in mind that in a cozy witch's practice you will never want to make a poppet of someone else without their permission first. A good example of this would be if you wish to help someone in some way. I like creating healing poppets when loved ones are in ill health or distressed in some way. I stay away from magic that brings harm to others.

WHAT YOU'LL NEED

Large piece of paper or card stock

Writing utensil

Scissors

Soft, pliable material, such as
cotton or felt (my first poppet
was a felt one)

Needle and thread

Pillow stuffing or straw

Herbs, oils, and crystal chips associated
with your intention

Note: When you do sympathetic magic like this, you want to be sure you never destroy the poppet. When you're finished, either give the poppet to the person it represents or bury it in the ground somewhere it will remain safe and sound.

METHOD

1. On the large piece of paper, draw the outline of a human figure and cut it out.

2. Fold your chosen material in half and place your paper human template on top. Carefully cut around the figure.

3. Sew the two cloth figures together, making sure to leave a small open area for stuffing it.

4. Turn the cloth figure right side out so the stitches are inside of the poppet. If you want a more rough-cut look, then feel free to keep the stitches on the outside and skip this step.

5. Stuff the cloth figure with pillow stuffing or straw and any magical correspondents you chose. As you stuff the herbs, oils, and/ or crystals inside, be sure to be thinking of the intention you're setting with each ingredient you push inside.

6. Sew the final few stitches in place to close all seams.

7. Your poppet is now ready for use. If this is a healing poppet, work with it at your altar with a light blue candle lit or a color you associate with healing. If it's a poppet to represent someone you wish protected, then work with it any way you'd do a magical working surrounding protection. If it's simply a poppet you've imbued with a special intention, then keep it on your altar or somewhere in your home or sacred space.

Cozy Witchy Pop Culture

Okay, I have to admit that I added this part just for fun. I know I talk at length on my podcast about my favorite witchy pop culture items, so I want to share many of those shows, movies, and musical artists here. In fact, over the years many people have asked me to create a list of my favorites, so there's really no better time than now . . . in this book.

Now, it won't be a surprise to many that I am a '90s baby!

Technically, I was born in the early '80s, but my memories of witchy television and movies were ones created in the '90s. I mean, how can I not love *Practical Magic* or the original *Sabrina the Teenage Witch* or the original *Charmed*? At one point I wanted to be Piper. Did I mention how much I loved *Halloweentown*, *Hocus Pocus*, *The Witches*, *Matilda* (she was truly magical), and one of my favorite, albeit cheesy, movies *Teen Witch*? If you haven't watched this classic, do yourself a favor and watch it. Cheesy witchiness at its finest. Oh, and as a side note, each time I emailed an updated draft of this manuscript to myself, I'd write *BOOK!* In the subject line and yell the word in the voice of Winifred Sanderson. Let's just say I got a few stares at my local Panera Bread and Starbucks.

Every fall I rewatch many of those favorites, but the show I come back to over and over again is *Good Witch*. I could go on and on about how I want to be Cassie Nightingale—and now that I've opened my brick-and-mortar Comfy Cozy Apothecary, I am getting close. Cassie is the epitome of subtle, intuitive witchcraft. She's warm, inviting, and compassionate, and she owns a charming bed-and-breakfast where she has a way of knowing just what her visitors need. She also runs her magical shop Bell, Book & Candle with that same intuitive prowess and innate kindness. Although many may find the show a little hokey, I absolutely love it as it, to me, is the perfect witchy comfort show.

And, of course, I can't forget about books. Although I do consume a fair amount of witchcraft and magic-related nonfiction, I also read a lot of magical fiction. I've always loved cozy mysteries and have written a few myself, but the fantasy cozy mysteries with witches and fairies and vampires are my favorite. I'm always surprised at how accurate the authors describe their characters' witchcraft practices and knowledge of herbs and spell work and incantations, and I often wonder if the authors themselves practice. If not, they either know someone who does or have thoroughly researched the topic.

Recently I was introduced to the cozy fantasy genre which, as you can imagine, is right up my alley as well. Some of my favorite titles so far have been *The House Witch*; *A Pinch of Magic*; *Midnight at the Blackbird Café*; *The Mermaid, the Witch, and the Sea*; and *Butter, Sugar Magic*. I'd eventually like to write a book in this genre myself, but I can only do so much.

I want to end this chapter by saying, even if you don't have time to practice your witchcraft on a daily basis, keep in mind that small rituals and reminders of our practice keep us connected to our magic. Sitting with a good book, watching witchy shows, pulling a card or two, pouring a cup of tea, noticing the animals that pop up in our lives—all these things connect us to our practice whether we realize it or not.

SOME OF MY FAVORITE COMFY COZY MAGICAL/ WITCHY MOVIES, TV SHOWS, AND BOOKS

TELEVISION SHOWS

✳ *Bewitched*

✳ *Charmed* (original series)

✳ *A Discovery of Witches*

✳ *The Good Witch* (movies and TV series)

* *Just Add Magic* (my son and I love watching this together)

* *Sabrina the Teenage Witch* (original series)

* *Witches of East End*

MOVIES

* *Bell, Book, and Candle*

* *Halloweentown* (my son loves this one too)

* *Hocus Pocus*

* *Kiki's Delivery Service*

* *The Little Witch*

* *Matilda*

* *Practical Magic*

* *Teen Witch*

* *The Witches*

* *The Witches of East Wick*

FICTION

* Bless Your Witch series by Amy Boyles

* *Butter, Sugar, Magic* by Jessica Rosenberg

* *Cackle* by Rachel Harrison

* *A Discovery of Witches* by Deborah Harkness

* Enchanted Bay Mystery series by Esme Addison

* *The Ex Hex* by Erin Sterling

* *The House Witch* by Delemhach

* Magical Bakery Mystery series by Bailey Cates

* *Midnight at the Blackbird Café* by Heather Webber

* *The Nature of Witches* by Rachel Griffin

* *The Once and Future Witches* by Alix E. Harrow

* Perfectly Proper Paranormal Museum Mystery series by Kirsten Weiss

* *A Pinch of Magic* by Michelle Harrison

* *Practical Magic* by Alice Hoffman

* *A Secret History of Witches* by Louisa Morgan

* *The Very Secret Society of Irregular Witches* by Sangu Mandanna

* *The Vine Witch* by Luanne G. Smith

* *The Witch's Daughter* by Paula Brackston

15

YOUR IDEAL MAGICAL SELF

WHEN I THINK BACK TO when I first wanted to be a witch nearly two and a half decades ago, never in a million years could I imagine being where I am now. There were many, many years of my life where I never let others know about my magical practice. I hid that part of myself out of fear, judgment, and uncertainty of whether I, myself, was *witchy* enough compared to others who'd practiced as long or longer than I had. And it wasn't until about a decade ago when I started to embrace the tenets that now make up my practice and find my authentic space in the witchy world. Over the years I found my ideal magical self by following the tenets outlined in this book, and it's my hope you've been able to do the same as well.

✳ ACCEPTANCE: I accept myself, my spiritual journey, and others who choose to practice how they see fit.

✳ SIMPLICITY: I create simple daily rituals to keep me in touch with my magic on a regular basis.

✳ REFLECTION: I reflect on my practice and explore the creative parts of my craft to make it better.

✳ DELIGHT: I find joy and meaning in my magical practice.

✳ WARMTH: My witchcraft practice promotes a warm spiritual environment filled with gratitude and compassion for myself and others.

✳ BALANCE: I work to find balance between my spiritual, physical, and emotional needs.

✳ INTUITION: I work hard at trusting myself and my intuition and my senses, and I trust my spirit team works with me.

If you look back at the tenet statements I wrote, they read and feel like mantras themselves and serve as important reminders as you embark, grow, or revisit your witchcraft journey. Write them down and take them with you wherever this magical journey of yours tracks.

Revisit the magical journal entries, prompt responses, and exercises, rituals, and spells you completed and created throughout this book. How do you feel about creating a witchcraft practice that is authentic to you? Are you well on your way, or do you need to take a pause to let everything soak in?

REFLECT IN YOUR JOURNAL

As a final activity, reflect on the following questions in your magical journal.

What does a magical practice look like to me?

What does it feel like to me?

How can I tap into the cozy parts of witchcraft?

What magical tools do I most enjoy working with?

What divination methods do I use often?

What divination methods would I like to try?

What clair sense is my strongest?

What are my favorite herbs to work with?

What are the most powerful crystals for me?

What intentions do I need to set for myself?

What magical workings can I do to reach these goals?

Just like any skill or hobby or journey, patience and practice is key. Find those small ways to touch your magic on a daily basis. Keep searching and learning. Read books that cover areas of witchcraft that appeal to you, but to grow even further, challenge yourself to read outside your comfort zone. That includes reading and shopping *outside* the witchy section. Head to the history section to read about ancient gods and goddesses or the history and myths of ancient cultures and religions. Take a peek at the psychology section to deepen your connection with your subconscious, meditation, and working with the shadow side of yourself. And look to the spirituality section to learn more about working with your intuition, clair senses, and spiritual self-care practices. Learning is key and can push us to reach deeper into ourselves and our practice.

When you feel ready, challenge yourself to step out of your comfort zone and switch up your daily ritual to keep your witchcraft fresh. Give that form of divination you've been curious about a try. Reach out to that local coven or meetup group of magic seekers. Head over to that local metaphysical shop and chat with the owner or sign up for that witchcraft conference you've been eying for years. And when you begin to feel intimidated or even judged by others' practices and perfectly curated witchy social media feeds, delete those apps and remind yourself that this witchcraft journey is yours and yours alone. Take anything you gained from reading and interacting with this book and apply it to your practice and leave behind anything that doesn't fit with your brand of magic.

Take your time. Establishing a witchcraft practice doesn't happen overnight. It's an ever-evolving journey of hits and misses, spells gone wrong, and intentions not coming to fruition. You'll try some things that resonate with you and others you'll never touch again. It took me nearly twenty years to find a practice that feels authentic to me, and no matter the thoughts and opinions of others, I know my craft is authentic and true to me because it's mine and mine alone. And don't forget that *practice makes magic*! Find small, meaningful ways to stay connected to your authentic brand of magic every single day.

Stay comfy, cozy, and witchy, my magical friends!

GLOSSARY OF MAGICAL CORRESPONDENCES

IN THIS GLOSSARY OF MAGICAL correspondences, you'll find the common magical associations with colors, animals, crystals, and herbs and plants. Calling in the energies of these items to support your work is a fundamental skill to practicing magic. Although some of these items and corresponding intentions may not resonate with you, they serve as useful tools when creating your own magical spells, recipes, rituals, and more. Always remember, your personal experiences are always the most meaningful and valid to you and your magical practice, so you can curate your own list of correspondences that resonate best with you!

Color Correspondences

BLACK: absorbs negativity, dispels negative energy, protection, mystery

BLUE: purifies energy, cleanses, communication, peace, healing, justice, throat chakra

BROWN: house and home, career, property, earth, stability

GOLD: the sun, energy, health, prosperity, masculine

GRAY: neutrality, calm, spirit work

GREEN: abundance, prosperity, healing, finances, nature, heart chakra

ORANGE: creativity, career movement, action, motivation, speed, sacral chakra

PINK: self-love, friendship, affection, heart chakra

PURPLE: intuition, magical power, spirituality

RED: energy, power, passion, love, action, root chakra

SILVER: the moon, divination, purity, feminine energy

TURQUOISE: water, ease, flow, calm, good health

VIOLET: meditation, spirituality, mysticism, psychic development, third-eye chakra

WHITE: purity, newness, wholeness, soothing, crown chakra

YELLOW: joy, clarity, travel, happy house and home, intelligence, confidence, solar plexus chakra

Animal Correspondences

BEAR: power, strength, steadfast, guardian

BEE: dedication, focus, prosperity

BLUE JAY: ancestor communication, intelligence, curiosity, family

BUTTERFLY: joy, grace, growth cycle, rebirth

CAT: curiosity, occult, magic

CROW: deceit, luck, trickster, fearless

DEER: alertness, gentleness, care, peace

DOG: loyalty, protection, perseverance

DOVE: love, faith, hope, peace

DRAGONFLY: change, adaptability, messages

FOX: agility, cunning, quickness, invisibility, cleverness

HORSE: stamina, power, freedom, travel

OWL: intuition, mystery, wisdom, observation

RABBIT: fertility, creativity, luck, abundance

RAVEN: healing, secrets, magic, omen

SNAKE: renewal, transformation, healing, magic

SPIDER: patience, creativity, storytelling, shadow

SQUIRREL: balance, hard work, positivity

WOLF: intuition, protection, teaching, discipline

Crystal Correspondences

AMETHYST: intuition, dreams, healing, psychic work

AVENTURINE: abundance, creativity, luck, study

BLACK TOURMALINE: absorbs negativity, grounding, protection

CITRINE: self-esteem, joy and happiness, abundance

CLEAR QUARTZ: amplifier, healing, protection

HOWLITE: sound sleep, meditation, calming

LAPIS LAZULI: communication, joy, healing, wisdom

OBSIDIAN: protection, releases fear and anger

ROSE QUARTZ: self-love, friendship, fidelity, love

SELENITE: cleanses other stones, clarity, lunar energy

SMOKY QUARTZ: grounding, transmutes negative energy, protection

SNOWFLAKE OBSIDIAN: grounding, balance, focus

SODALITE: healing, peace, wisdom, meditation

TIGER'S-EYE: money, protection, energy, luck

YELLOW CALCITE: sun energy, protection

Herb and Plant Correspondences

BASIL: protection, abundance

BAY LEAF: success, prosperity

CEDAR: cleansing, clarity, protection, meditation

CINNAMON: warmth, healing, passion, joy, spirituality

DANDELION: health, healing, happiness

EUCALYPTUS: happiness, energizing, purification, healing

FRANKINCENSE: meditation work, lifting vibrations and energy

LAVENDER: calm, peace, happiness, love

LEMON BALM: abundance, prosperity, healing, friendship

MUGWORT: divination, vivid dreams

PEPPERMINT: focus, study, travel, psychic powers, healing

ROSE: healing, love, luck, friendship, heart-opening

ROSEMARY: sleep, cognitive abilities, purification, protection

SAGE: cleansing, wisdom, longevity, immortality

A NOTE
on the
COVER

EACH FLOWER, LEAF, MUSHROOM, AND TWIG on this cover, as well as all of the lettering, was crocheted with the help of a tiny hook and cotton thread inherited from my grandmother. I love the idea of being able to use such simple materials to produce rich, textural imagery and definitely feel a spark of magic when all of the elements come together as a whole. It's a kind of witchcraft in itself and makes me feel closer to nature, my ancestors, and the ancient urge to tell a story with one's hands.

—*Caitlin McCormack*